ESSENTIAL
Introduction to Computers
and How to Purchase, Install, and Maintain a Personal Computer

OBJECTIVES

After completing this material, you will be able to:

- Define the term computer and discuss the four basic computer operations: input, processing, output, and storage

- Define data and information

- Explain the principal components of the computer and their use

- Describe the use of floppy disks, hard disks, and other storage media

- Discuss computer software and explain the difference between system software and application software

- Identify several types of personal computer application software

- Discuss computer communications channels and equipment and the Internet and World Wide Web

- Explain how to purchase, install, and maintain a personal computer

- Define e-commerce

Everyday, computers impact how individuals work and how they live. The use of personal computers continues to increase and has made computing available to almost anyone. In addition, advances in communications technology allow people to use personal computers to access and send information easily and quickly to other computers and computer users. At home, at work, and in the field, computers are helping people to do their work faster, more accurately, and in some cases, in ways that previously would not have been possible.

Computers

Visit the Introduction to Computers WEB LINK page (scsite.com/ic5/weblink) and click Computers.

WHAT IS A COMPUTER?

A **computer** is an electronic device, operating under the control of instructions stored in its own memory unit, that can accept data (input), manipulate the data according to specified rules (process), produce information (output) from the processing, and store the results for future use. Generally, the term is used to describe a collection of devices that function together as a system. An example of the devices that make up a personal computer is shown in Figure 1.

WHAT DOES A COMPUTER DO?

Whether small or large, computers can perform four general operations. These operations comprise the **information processing cycle** and are input, process, output, and storage. Collectively, these operations describe the procedures a computer performs to process data into information and store it for future use.

FIGURE 1 Common computer hardware components include a keyboard, mouse, microphone, scanner, digital camera, PC camera, printer, monitor, speakers, system unit, disk drives, card reader, and modem.

CD/DVD drive (storage)

PC video camera (input)

floppy disk drive (storage)

monitor (output)

hard disk drive (storage)

screen

modem (communications)

speaker (output)

speaker (output)

mouse (input)

system unit (processor, memory, and storage)

keyboard (input)

scanner (input)

printer (output)

microphone (input)

card reader (storage)

digital camera (input)

All computer processing requires **data**. Data is a collection of raw facts, figures, and symbols, such as numbers, words, images, video, and sounds, given to a computer during the input operation. Computers manipulate data to create information. **Information** is data that is organized, meaningful, and useful. During the output operation, the information that has been created is put into some form, such as a printed report, or it can be written to computer storage for future use. As shown in Figure 2, a computer processes several data items to produce a paycheck. Another example of information is a grade report, which is generated from data items such as a student name, course names, and course grades.

People who use the computer directly or use the information it provides are called **computer users**, **end users**, or sometimes, just **users**.

WHY IS A COMPUTER SO POWERFUL?

A computer derives its power from its capability to perform the information processing cycle with amazing speed, reliability (low failure rate), and accuracy; its capacity to store huge amounts of data and information; and its ability to communicate with other computers.

HOW DOES A COMPUTER KNOW WHAT TO DO?

For a computer to perform operations, it must be given a detailed set of instructions that tells it exactly what to do. These instructions are called a **computer program**, or **software**. Before processing for a specific job begins, the computer program corresponding to that job is stored in the computer. Once the program is stored, the computer can begin to operate by executing the program's first instruction. The computer executes one program instruction after another until the job is complete.

Information

Visit the Introduction to Computers WEB LINK page (scsite.com/ic5/ weblink) and click Information.

Computer Programs

Visit the Introduction to Computers WEB LINK page (scsite.com/ic5/ weblink) and click Computer Programs.

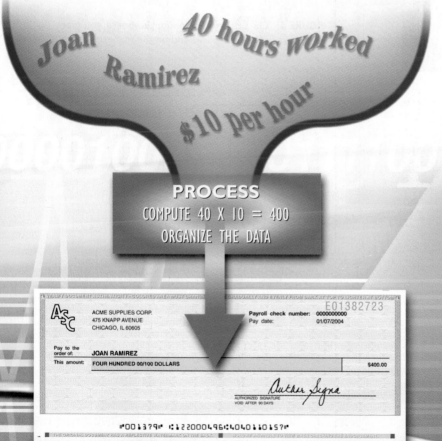

FIGURE 2 A computer processes data into information. In this example, the employee name, number of hours worked, and hourly pay rate each represent data. The computer processes these items to produce the desired information, in this case, a paycheck.

Input Devices

Visit the Introduction to Computers WEB LINK page (scsite.com/ic5/weblink) and click Input Devices.

WHAT ARE THE COMPONENTS OF A COMPUTER?

To understand how computers process data into information, you need to examine the primary components of the computer. The six primary components of a computer are input devices, the processor (control unit and arithmetic/logic unit), memory, output devices, storage devices, and communications devices. The processor, memory, and storage devices are housed in a box-like case called the **system unit**. Figure 3 shows the flow of data, information, and instructions between the first five components mentioned. The next six sections describe these primary components.

FIGURE 3 Most devices connected to the computer communicate with the processor to carry out a task. When a user starts a program, for example, its instructions transfer from a storage device to memory. Data needed by programs enters memory either from an input device or a storage device. The control unit interprets and executes instructions in memory and the ALU performs calculations on the data in memory. Resulting information is stored in memory, from which it can be sent to an output device or a storage device for future access, as needed.

INPUT DEVICES

An **input device** is any hardware component that allows you to enter data, programs, commands, and user responses into a computer. Depending on your particular application and requirement, the input device you use may vary. Popular input devices include the keyboard, mouse, digital camera, scanner, and microphone. The two primary input devices used are the keyboard and the mouse. This section discusses both of these input devices.

The Keyboard

A keyboard is an input device that contains keys you press to enter data into the computer. A desktop computer keyboard (Figure 4) typically has 101 to 105 keys. Keyboards for smaller computers, such as notebooks, contain fewer keys. A computer keyboard includes keys that allow you to type letters of the alphabet, numbers, spaces, punctuation marks, and other symbols such as the dollar sign ($) and asterisk (*). A keyboard also contains other keys that allow you to enter data and instructions into the computer.

FIGURE 4 On a desktop computer keyboard, you type using keys in the typing area and on the numeric keypad.

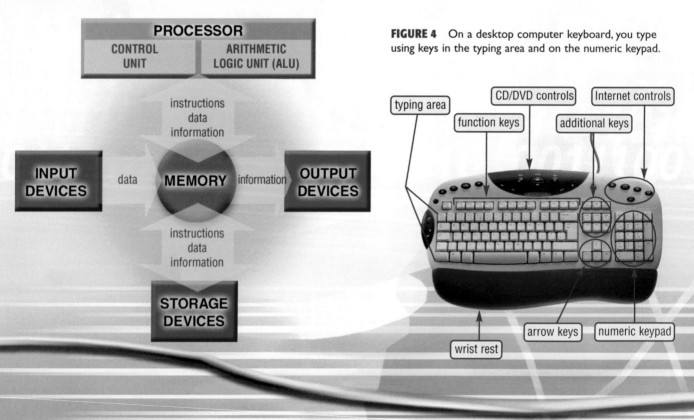

Most handheld computers (left in Figure 5) use an onscreen keyboard. With handheld computers, you use a stylus to select keys on the onscreen keyboard. A notebook computer (right in Figure 5) has the keyboard built into the top of the unit.

FIGURE 5 A handheld computer (left) employs an onscreen keyboard and stylus. A notebook computer (right) has the keyboard built into the unit.

The Mouse

A **mouse** (Figure 6) is a pointing device that fits comfortably under the palm of your hand. With a mouse, you control the movement of the **pointer**, often called the **mouse pointer**, on the screen and make selections from the screen. A mouse has one to five buttons. The bottom of a mouse is flat and contains a mechanism (optical sensor or ball) that detects movement of the mouse.

Notebook computers come with a pointing device built into the keyboard (Figure 7) so that you can select items on the screen without requiring additional desktop space.

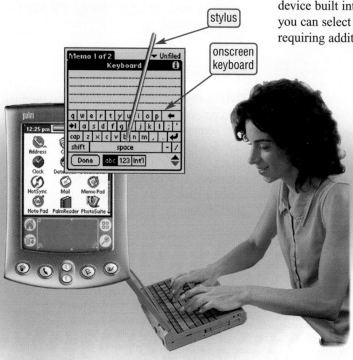

FIGURE 7 Some notebook computers include a pointing device to allow a user to control the movement of the pointer.

FIGURE 6 This optical mouse uses an optical sensor. It also includes buttons to push with your thumb that enable forward and backward navigation through Web pages.

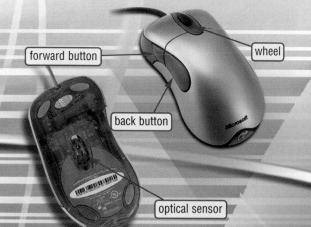

Processor

Visit the Introduction to Computers WEB LINK page (scsite.com/ic5/ weblink) and click Processor.

Memory

Visit the Introduction to Computers WEB LINK page (scsite.com/ic5/ weblink) and click Memory.

Output Devices

Visit the Introduction to Computers WEB LINK page (scsite.com/ic5/ weblink) and click Output Devices.

PROCESSOR

The **processor**, also called the **central processing unit** (**CPU**), interprets and carries out the basic instructions that operate a computer. The processor is made up of the control unit and arithmetic/logic unit (Figure 3 on page COM-4). The **control unit** interprets the instructions. The **arithmetic/logic unit** performs the logical and arithmetic processes. The personal computer processors shown in Figure 8 can fit in the palm of your hand. The high-end processors contain 42 million transistors and are capable of performing some operations 10 million times in a tenth of a second, or in the time it takes to blink your eye.

MEMORY

Memory, also called **random access memory**, or **RAM**, consists of electronic components that store instructions waiting to be executed by the processor, data needed by those instructions, and the results of processed data (information). Memory usually consists of one or more chips on the motherboard in the computer. The **motherboard** (Figure 9), sometimes

called a **system board**, is the main circuit board in the computer to which many electronic components are attached.

The amount of memory in computers typically is measured in kilobytes or megabytes. One **kilobyte** (**K or KB**) equals approximately 1,000 memory locations and one **megabyte** (**M or MB**) equals approximately one million memory locations. A **memory location**, or **byte**, usually stores one character. Therefore, a computer with 96 MB of memory can store approximately 96 million characters. One megabyte can hold approximately 500 pages of text information.

OUTPUT DEVICES

Output devices make the information resulting from processing available for use. The output from computers can be presented in many forms, such as a printed report or displaying it on a screen. When a computer is used for processing tasks such as word processing, spreadsheets, or database management, the two output devices more commonly used are the printer and a display device.

FIGURE 8 Less powerful personal computers have a Celeron processor. Higher-performance personal computers use Athlon XP and Pentium processors.

Celeron™

Athlon XP™

Pentium™

FIGURE 9 The motherboard is housed in the system unit of a desktop personal computer. It contains many electronic components, including adapter cards, a processor chip, memory chips, memory slots, and expansion slots. Memory slots hold memory cards (modules) and expansion slots hold adapter cards.

sound card

video card

processor

memory chips

modem card

network card

expansion slots for adapter cards

motherboard

memory slots

Printers

Printers used with computers can be either impact printers or nonimpact printers. An **impact printer** prints by striking an inked ribbon against the paper. One type of impact printer used with personal computers is the dot matrix printer (Figure 10).

Nonimpact printers, such as ink-jet printers (Figure 11) and laser printers (Figure 12), form characters by means other than striking a ribbon against paper. One advantage of using a nonimpact printer is that it can print higher-quality text and graphics than an impact printer, such as the dot matrix. Nonimpact printers also do a better job printing different fonts, are quieter, and can print in color. The popular and affordable ink-jet printer forms a character or graphic by using a nozzle that sprays drops of ink onto the page.

Ink-jet printers produce excellent images. The speed of an ink-jet printer is measured by the number of pages per minute (ppm) it can print. Most ink-jet printers print from three to nineteen pages per minute. Graphics and colors print at the slower rate.

Laser printers (Figure 12) work similarly to a copying machine by converting data from the computer into a beam of light that is focused on a photoconductor drum, forming the images to be printed. Laser printers produce high-quality black-and-white or color output and are used for applications that combine text and graphics such as desktop publishing. Laser printers for personal computers can cost from a few hundred dollars to several thousand dollars. The more expensive the laser printer, the more pages it can print per minute.

FIGURE 10 Dot matrix printers are capable of handling wide paper and printing multipart forms.

FIGURE 12 Laser printers are used with personal computers, as well as larger computers.

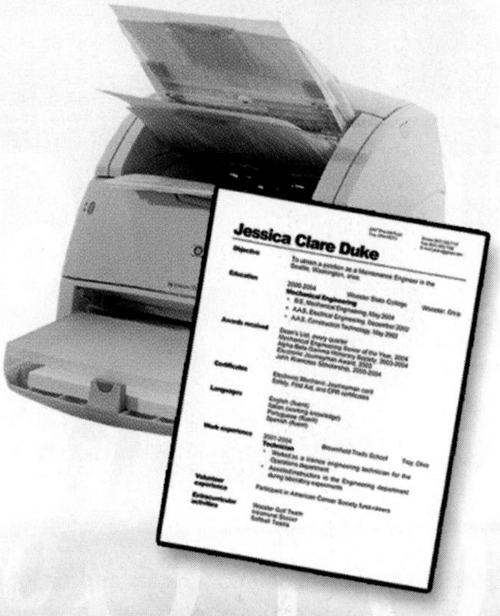

FIGURE 11 Ink-jet printers are the most popular type of printer used in the home.

Display Devices

A display device is an output device that visually conveys text, graphics, and video information. A **monitor** is a plastic or metal case that houses a display device. There are two basic types of monitors, CRT and LCD. The television-like **CRT (cathode ray tube)** monitor shown on the left in Figure 13 is the most common display device used with desktop computers. The **LCD monitor**, also called a **flat panel monitor**, shown on the right in Figure 13 uses a liquid display crystal, similar to a digital watch, to produce images on the screen. The flat panel monitor, although more expensive than the CRT monitor, takes up much less desk space. The surface of the screen of either a CRT monitor or LCD monitor is composed of individual picture elements called **pixels**. A screen set to a resolution of 800 x 600 pixels has a total of 480,000 pixels. Each pixel can be illuminated to form parts of a character or graphic shape on the screen.

Mobile computers, such as notebook computers and Tablet PCs, and mobile devices, such as PDAs and smart phones, have LCD screens (Figure 14).

FIGURE 13 The CRT monitor (left) and flat panel monitor (right) are used with desktop computers. The flat panel monitor is much thinner and weighs less than a CRT monitor.

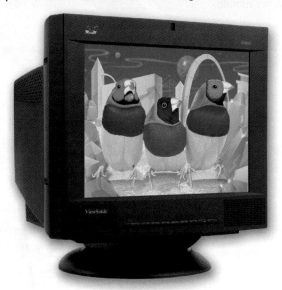
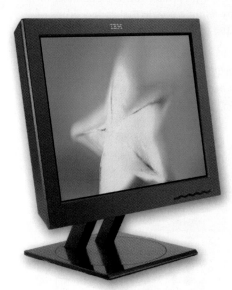

FIGURE 14 Notebook computers and Tablet PCs have color LCD screens. Some PDAs have color displays and a few smart phones even have color displays.

STORAGE DEVICES

Storage devices are used to store instructions, data, and information when they are not being used in memory. Six common types of storage devices are floppy disks, zip disks, optical discs, tape, and miniature storage media. Figure 15 shows how different types of storage media and memory compare in terms of relative speeds and uses.

Floppy Disks

A **floppy disk**, or **diskette**, is a portable, inexpensive storage medium that consists of a thin, circular, flexible plastic disk with a magnetic coating enclosed in a square-shaped plastic shell (Figure 16). The most widely used floppy disk is 3.5 inches wide and typically can store up to 1.44 megabytes of data or 1,474,560 characters. Although the exterior of the 3.5-inch disk is not floppy, users still refer to them as floppy disks.

A floppy disk is a **portable storage medium**. When discussing a storage medium, the term portable means you can remove the medium from one computer and carry it to another computer. For example, you can insert a floppy disk into and remove it from a floppy disk drive on many types of computers (Figure 17). A **floppy disk drive** is a device that can read from and write to a floppy disk.

FIGURE 16 In a 3.5-inch floppy disk, a thin, circular, flexible Mylar film is enclosed between two liners. A piece of metal called a shutter covers an opening to the recording surface in the rigid plastic shell.

FIGURE 15 A comparison of different types of storage media and memory in terms of relative speed and uses. Memory is faster than storage, but is expensive and not practical for all storage requirements. Storage is less expensive than memory.

faster transfer rates ↑		Stores...
Primary Storage	Memory (most RAM)	Items waiting to be interpreted and executed by the processor
Secondary Storage	Hard Disk	Operating system, application software, user data and information
	CDs and DVDs	Software, backups, movies, music
	Miniature Storage Media	Digital pictures or small files to be transported
	Tape	Backups
	Floppy Disk	Small files to be transported
slower access times ↓		

FIGURE 17 On a personal computer, you insert and remove a floppy disk from a floppy disk drive.

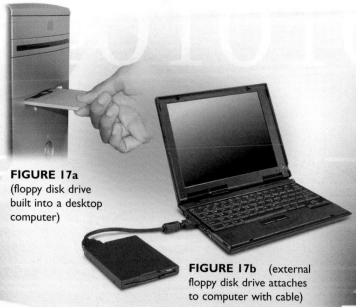

FIGURE 17a (floppy disk drive built into a desktop computer)

FIGURE 17b (external floppy disk drive attaches to computer with cable)

A floppy disk is a type of magnetic disk, which means it uses magnetic patterns to store items such as data, instructions, and information on the disk's surface. Most magnetic disks are read/write storage media; that is, you can access (read) data from and place (write) data on a magnetic disk any number of times, just as you can with an audiocassette tape. Most floppy disks that you purchase are already formatted. If they are not formatted, then before you can write on a new floppy disk, it must be formatted.

Formatting is the process of preparing a disk (floppy disk or hard disk) for reading and writing by organizing the disk into storage locations called tracks and sectors (Figure 18). A **track** is a narrow recording band that forms a full circle on the surface of the disk. The disk's storage locations then are divided into pie-shaped sections, which break the tracks into small arcs called sectors. A **sector** is capable of holding 512 bytes of data. A typical floppy disk stores data on both sides and has 80 tracks on each side of the recording surface with 18 sectors per track.

Data stored in sectors on a floppy disk must be retrieved and placed into memory to be processed. The time required to access and retrieve data is called the **access time**. The access time for floppy disks varies from about 175 milliseconds (one millisecond equals 1/1000 of a second) to approximately 300 milliseconds. On average, data stored in a single sector on a floppy disk can be retrieved in approximately 1/15 to 1/3 of a second.

Zip Disks

A **Zip disk** is a type of portable magnetic media that can store up to 750 MB of data. Zip disks can be built-in to the system unit or it can be external (Figure 19). The Zip disk can hold about 500 times more than a standard floppy disk. These large capacities make it easy to transport many files or large items such as graphics, audio, or video files. Another popular use of Zip disks is to back up important data and information. A **backup** is a duplicate of a file, program, or disk that you can use in case the original is lost, damaged, or destroyed.

Hard Disks

Another form of storage is a hard disk. A **hard disk** (Figure 20) consists of one or more rigid metal platters coated with a metal oxide material that allows data to be recorded magnetically. Although hard disks are available in removable cartridge form, most disks cannot be removed from the computer. As with floppy disks, the data on hard disks is recorded on a series of tracks. The tracks are divided into sectors when the disk is formatted.

Hard Disks
Visit the Introduction to Computers WEB LINK page (scsite.com/ic5/weblink) and click Hard Disks.

FIGURE 18 Tracks form circles on the surface of a disk. The disk's storage locations are divided into pie-shaped sections, which break the tracks into small arcs called sectors.

FIGURE 19 An external Zip drive has a cable that plugs into a port on a system unit.

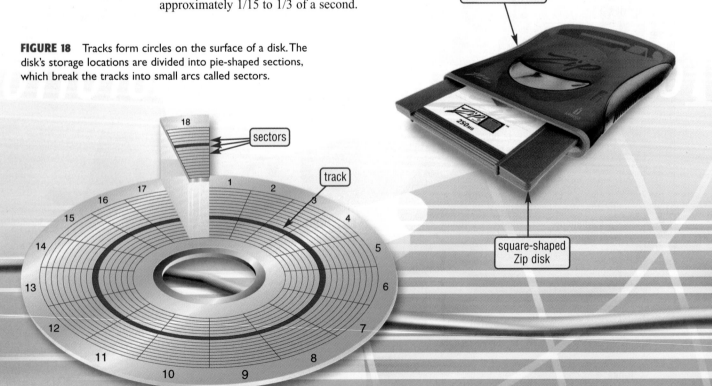

The hard disk platters spin at a high rate of speed, typically 5,400 to 7,200 revolutions per minute. When reading data from the disk, the read head senses the magnetic spots that are recorded on the disk along the various tracks and transfers that data to memory. When writing, the data is transferred from memory and is stored as magnetic spots on the tracks on the recording surface of one or more of the disk platters. When reading or writing, the read/write heads on a hard disk drive do not actually touch the surface of the disk.

The number of platters permanently mounted on the spindle of a hard disk varies. On most drives, each surface of the platter can be used to store data. Thus, if a hard disk drive uses one platter, two surfaces are available for data. If the drive uses two platters, four sets of read/write heads read and record data from the four surfaces. Storage capacities of internally mounted fixed disks for personal computers range from one billion characters to more than 200 billion characters. One billion bytes are called a **gigabyte (GB)**. Typical hard disk sizes range from 40 GB to 200 GB.

Optical Discs

An **optical disc** is a storage medium that consists of a flat, round, portable, metal storage medium that usually is 4.75 inches in diameter and less than 1/20 of an inch thick. Two types of optical discs are CD and DVD. Just about every desktop computer and notebook computer includes some type of compact disc drive installed in a drive bay. Many computers come with both a CD and DVD drive. These drives read compact discs, including audio discs.

Optical Discs
Visit the Introduction to Computers WEB LINK page (scsite.com/ic5/weblink) and click Optical Discs.

FIGURE 20   The hard disk in a desktop computer is enclosed inside an airtight, sealed case inside the system unit.

hard disk installed in system unit

On a CD or DVD drive, you push a button to slide out a tray, insert your compact disc with the label side up, and then push the same button to close the tray (Figure 21). Other convenient features on most of these drives include a volume control button and a headphone jack so you can use stereo headphones to listen to audio without disturbing others nearby.

Compact discs are available in a variety of formats, including CD-ROM, CD-R, CD-RW, DVD-ROM, and DVD+RW.

CD-ROMs
A **CD-ROM** (pronounced SEE-DEE-rom), or **compact disc read-only memory**, is a type of optical disc that uses the same laser technology as audio CDs for recording music. In addition to audio, a CD-ROM can contain text, graphics, and video. The manufacturer writes, or records, the contents of standard CD-ROMs. You can only read the contents of these discs. That is, you cannot erase or modify their contents — hence the name read-only.

A typical CD-ROM holds from 650 MB to 1 GB of data, instructions, and information. This is 450 to 700 times more than you can store on a 3.5-inch floppy disk.

CD-R and CD-RW
A **CD-R** (**compact disc-recordable**) is a multisession optical disc onto which you can record your own items such as text, graphics, and audio. With a CD-R, you can write on part of the disc at one time and another part at a later time. Once you have recorded the CD-R, you can read from it as many times as you wish. You can write on each part only one time, and you cannot erase the disc's contents. Most CD-ROM drives can read a CD-R.

A **CD-RW** (**compact disc-rewritable**) is an erasable disc you can write on multiple times. Originally called an erasable CD (CD-E), a CD-RW overcomes the major disadvantage of CD-R discs, which is that you can write on them only once. With CD-RWs, the disc acts like a floppy or hard disk, allowing you to write and rewrite data, instructions, and information onto it multiple times.

DVDs
Although CDs have huge storage capacities, even a CD is not large enough for many of today's complex programs. Some software, for example, is sold on five or more CDs. To meet these tremendous storage requirements, some software companies have moved from CDs to the larger DVD — a technology that can be used to store large amounts of text and even cinema-like videos (Figure 22).

DVD-ROMs
Visit the Introduction to Computers WEB LINK page (scsite.com/ic5/weblink) and click DVD-ROMs.

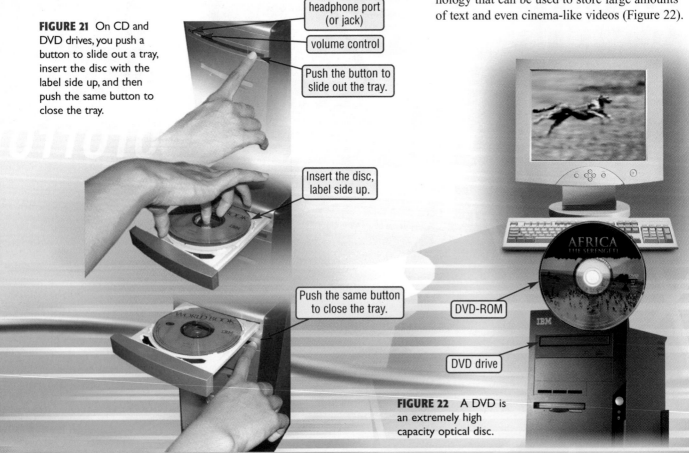

FIGURE 21 On CD and DVD drives, you push a button to slide out a tray, insert the disc with the label side up, and then push the same button to close the tray.

headphone port (or jack)

volume control

Push the button to slide out the tray.

Insert the disc, label side up.

Push the same button to close the tray.

DVD-ROM

DVD drive

FIGURE 22 A DVD is an extremely high capacity optical disc.

A **DVD-ROM (digital video disc-ROM)** is a very high capacity optical disc capable of storing from 4.7 GB to 17 GB — more than enough to hold a telephone book containing every resident in the United States. As with the CD-ROM format, you cannot write to an optical disc that uses the DVD-ROM format. You can only read from it.

With optical discs that use the **DVD+RW (DVD-rewriteable)** format, a user can erase and record more than a 1,000 times. One major use of the high-capacity DVD+RW format is the ability to edit videos read from a video camera or VCR, stored and edited on your computer, and then written to a DVD+RW disc.

Tape

Tape is a magnetically coated ribbon of plastic housed in a tape cartridge (Figure 23) capable of storing large amounts of data and information at a low cost. A tape drive is used to read from and write to a tape. Tape is primarily used for long-term storage and backup.

Miniature Storage Media

Miniature storage media is rewritable media usually in the form of a flash memory card. Flash memory cards are solid-state devices, which means they consist entirely of electronics (chips, wires, etc.) and contain no moving parts. Miniature storage media (Figure 24) is the primary storage used with PDAs, digital cameras, music players, and smart phones to store digital images, music, or documents.

Flash Memory Cards

Visit the Introduction to Computers WEB LINK page (scsite.com/ic5/weblink) and click Flash Memory Cards.

FIGURE 24 Digital cameras, music players, PDAs, smart phones, and notebook computers use miniature mobile storage media.

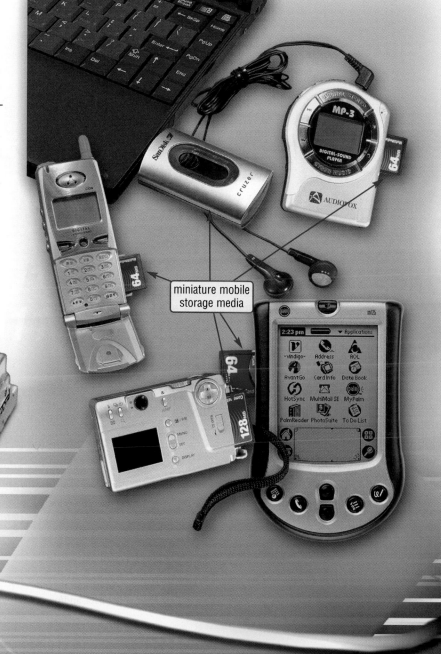

miniature mobile storage media

FIGURE 23 A tape cartridge and a tape drive.

COMMUNICATIONS DEVICES

A **communications device** is a hardware component that enables a computer to send (transmit) and receive data, instructions, and information to and from one or more computers. A widely used communication device is the modem (Figure 1 on page COM-2).

Communications occur over **transmission media**, such as cables, telephone lines, cellular radio networks, satellites. Some transmission media, such as satellites and cellular radio networks, are wireless, which means they have no physical lines or wires. People around the world use computers and communications devices to communicate with each other using one or more transmission media.

COMPUTER SOFTWARE

Computer software is the key to productive use of computers. With the correct software, a computer can become a valuable tool. Software can be categorized into two types: system software and application software.

System Software

System software consists of programs to control the operations of computer equipment. An important part of system software is a set of programs called the operating system. Instructions in the **operating system** tell the computer how to perform the functions of loading, storing, and executing an application program and how to transfer data. For a computer to operate, an operating system must be stored in the computer's memory. When a computer is turned on, the operating system is loaded into the computer's memory from auxiliary storage. This process is called **booting**.

Today, most computers use an operating system that has a **graphical user interface (GUI)** that provides visual cues such as icon symbols to help the user. Each icon represents an application such as word processing, or a file or document where data is stored. Microsoft Windows (Figure 25) is a widely used graphical operating system. Apple Macintosh computers also have a graphical user interface operating system.

Application Software

Application software consists of programs that tell a computer how to produce information. Some widely used application software includes personal information manager, project management, accounting, computer-aided design, desktop publishing, paint/image editing, audio and video editing, multimedia authoring, Web page authoring, personal finance, legal, tax preparation, home design/landscaping, educational, reference, and entertainment (games, simulations, etc.). As shown in Figure 26, you often purchase application software from a store that sells computer products.

Personal computer users often use application software. Some of the more commonly used applications are word processing, electronic spreadsheet, presentation graphics, database, communications, and electronic mail software. Some software packages, such as Microsoft Office, also include access to the World Wide Web as an integral part of the application.

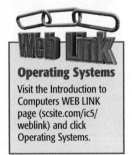

Operating Systems

Visit the Introduction to Computers WEB LINK page (scsite.com/ic5/weblink) and click Operating Systems.

FIGURE 25 A graphical user interface such as Microsoft Windows makes the computer easier to use. The small pictures, or symbols, on the screen are called icons. Icons represent a program or data the user can choose. A window is a rectangular area of the screen that is used to display a program, data, and/or information.

Word Processing

Word processing software (Figure 27) is used to create, edit, format, and print documents. A key advantage of word processing software is that users easily can make changes in documents, such as correcting spelling, changing margins, and adding, deleting, or relocating entire paragraphs. These changes would be difficult and time consuming to make using manual methods such as a typewriter. With a word processor, documents can be printed quickly and accurately and easily stored on a disk for future use. Word processing software is oriented toward working with text, but most word processing packages also can include numeric and graphic information.

FIGURE 26 Stores that sell computer products have shelves stocked with software for sale.

Spreadsheet

Electronic spreadsheet software (Figure 28) allows the user to add, subtract, and perform user-defined calculations on rows and columns of numbers. These numbers can be changed, and the spreadsheet quickly recalculates the new results. Electronic spreadsheet software eliminates the tedious recalculations required with manual methods. Spreadsheet information frequently is converted into a graphic form, such as charts. Graphics capabilities now are included in most spreadsheet packages.

FIGURE 27 Word processing software is used to create letters, memos, and other documents.

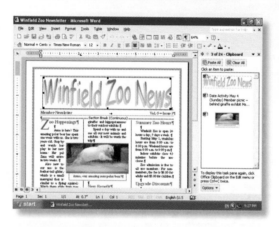

FIGURE 28 Electronic Spreadsheet software frequently is used by people who work with numbers. The user enters the data and the formulas to be used on the data, and the computer calculates the results.

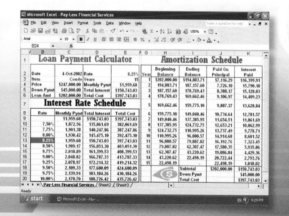

Word Processing Software

Visit the Introduction to Computers WEB LINK page (scsite.com/ic5/weblink) and click Word Processing Software.

Spreadsheet Software

Visit the Introduction to Computers WEB LINK page (scsite.com/ic5/weblink) and click Spreadsheet Software.

Database Software

Visit the Introduction to Computers WEB LINK page (scsite.com/ic5/weblink) and click Database Software.

Presentation Graphics Software

Visit the Introduction to Computers WEB LINK page (scsite.com/ic5/weblink) and click Presentation Graphics Software.

Database **Database software** (Figure 29) allows the user to enter, retrieve, and update data in an organized and efficient manner. These software packages have flexible inquiry and reporting capabilities that let users access the data in different ways and create custom reports that include some or all of the information in the database.

Presentation Graphics **Presentation graphics software** (Figure 30) allows the user to create documents called slides to be used in making presentations. Using special projection devices, the slides are projected directly from the computer.

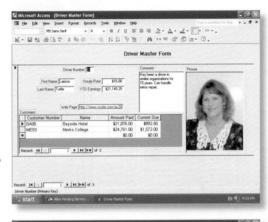

FIGURE 29 Database software allows the user to enter, retrieve, and update data in an organized and efficient manner.

FIGURE 30 Presentation graphics software allows the user to create documents called slides for use in presentations.

NETWORKS AND THE INTERNET

A **network** is a collection of computers and devices connected via communications media and devices such as cables, telephone lines, modems, or other means.

Computers are networked together so users can share resources, such as hardware devices, software programs, data, and information. Sharing resources saves time and money. For example, instead of purchasing one printer for every computer in a company, the firm can connect a single printer and all computers via a network (Figure 31); the network enables all of the computers to access the same printer.

Most business computers are networked together. These networks can be relatively small or quite extensive. A network that connects computers in a limited geographic area, such as a school computer laboratory, office, or group of buildings, is called a **local area network** (**LAN**). A network that covers a large geographical area, such as one that connects the district offices of a national corporation, is called a **wide area network** (**WAN**) (Figure 32).

FIGURE 31 This local area network (LAN) enables two or more separate computers to share the same printer.

client client

printer server

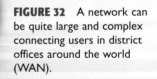

FIGURE 32 A network can be quite large and complex connecting users in district offices around the world (WAN).

The Internet

The world's largest network is the **Internet**, which is a worldwide collection of networks that links together millions of computers by means of modems, telephone lines, cables, and other communications devices and media. With an abundance of resources and data accessible via the Internet, more than 600 million users around the world are making use of the Internet for a variety of reasons (Figure 33). Some of these reasons include the following:

- Sending messages to other connected users (e-mail)

- Accessing a wealth of information, such as news, maps, airline schedules, and stock market data

- Shopping for goods and services

- Meeting or conversing with people around the world

- Accessing sources of entertainment and leisure, such as online games, magazines, and vacation planning guides

Most users connect to the Internet in one of two ways: through an Internet service provider or through an online service provider. An **Internet service provider** (**ISP**) is an organization that supplies connections to the Internet for a monthly fee. Like an ISP, an **online service provider** (**OSP**) provides access to the Internet, but it also provides a variety of other specialized content and services such as financial data, hardware and software guides, news, weather, legal information, and other similar commodities. For this reason, the fees for using an online service usually are slightly higher than fees for using an ISP. Two popular online services are America Online and The Microsoft Network.

The World Wide Web

One of the more popular segments of the Internet is the **World Wide Web**, also called the **Web**, which contains billions of documents called Web pages. A **Web page** is a document that contains text, graphics, sound, and/or video, and has built-in connections, or hyperlinks, to other Web documents. Web pages are stored on computers throughout the world. A **Web site** is a related collection of Web pages. You access and view Web pages using a software program called a **Web browser**. A Web page has a unique address, called a **Uniform Resource Locator** (**URL**).

Internet
Visit the Introduction to Computers WEB LINK page (scsite.com/ic5/ weblink) and click Internet.

FIGURE 33 Users access the Internet for a variety of reasons: to send messages to other connected users, to access a wealth of information, to shop for goods and services, to meet or converse with people around the world, and for entertainment.

World Wide Web

Visit the Introduction to Computers WEB LINK page (scsite.com/ic5/weblink) and click World Wide Web.

E-Commerce

Visit the Introduction to Computers WEB LINK page (scsite.com/ic5/weblink) and click E-Commerce.

As shown in Figure 34, a URL consists of a protocol, domain name, and sometimes the path to a specific Web page or location in a Web page. Most Web page URLs begin with **http://**, which stands for hypertext transfer protocol, the communications standard used to transfer pages on the Web. The domain name identifies the Web site, which is stored on a Web server. A **Web server** is a computer that delivers (serves) requested Web pages.

Electronic Commerce

When you conduct business activities online, you are participating in **electronic commerce**, also known as **e-commerce**. These commercial activities include shopping, investing, and any other venture that represents a business transaction. Today, three types of e-commerce exist: business to consumer, consumer to consumer, and business to business. **Business to consumer (B2C)** involves the sale of goods to the general public. **Consumer to consumer (C2C)** involves one consumer selling directly to another. **Business to business (B2B)** provides goods and services to other businesses.

FIGURE 34 One method of connecting to the Web and displaying a Web page.

STEP 1 Use your computer and modem to make a local telephone call to an internet service provider.

STEP 2 With your browser on the screen, enter the address, or URL, of the Web site you want to visit.

protocol | domain name | path | Web page name

http://www.jnj.com/careers/index.html

STEP 3 The Web browser locates the web site for the entered address and displays a Web page on your screen.

How to Purchase, Install, and Maintain a Personal Computer

At some point, perhaps while you are taking this course, you may decide to buy a personal computer. The decision is an important one, which will require an investment of both time and money. As with many buyers, you may have little computer experience and find yourself unsure of how to proceed. You can get started by talking to your friends, coworkers, and instructors about their computers. What type of computers did they buy? Why? For what purposes do they use their computers? You also should answer the following four questions to help narrow your choices to a specific computer type, before reading the Buyer's Guide guidelines for purchasing a desktop computer, notebook computer, Tablet PC, or PDA.

Do you want a desktop or mobile computer?

A desktop computer (Figure 35a) is designed as a stationary device that sits on or below a desk or table in a location such as a home, office, or dormitory room. A desktop computer must be plugged into an electrical outlet to operate. A mobile computer or device, such as a notebook computer (Figure 35b), Tablet PC (Figure 35c), and PDA (Figure 35d), is smaller, more portable, and has a battery that allows you to operate it for a period without an electrical outlet.

Desktop computers are a good option if you work mostly in one place and have plenty of space in your work area. Desktop computers generally give you more performance for your money and are easier to upgrade than mobile computers.

Increasingly, more desktop computer users are buying notebook computers to take advantage of their portability to work in the library, while traveling, and at home. The past disadvantages of notebook computers, such as lower processor speeds, poor-quality monitors, weight, short battery life, and significantly higher prices, have all but disappeared when compared with desktop computers.

If you are thinking of using a mobile computer to take notes in class or in business meetings, then consider a Tablet PC with handwriting and drawing capabilities. Typically, note-taking involves writing text notes and drawing charts, schematics, and other illustrations. By allowing you to write and draw directly on the screen with a digital pen, a Tablet PC eliminates the distracting sound of the notebook keyboard tapping and allows you to capture drawings. Some notebook computers can convert to Tablet PCs.

FIGURE 35

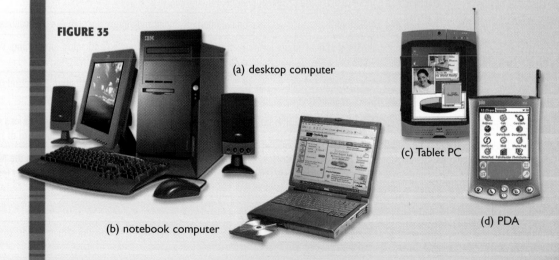

(a) desktop computer

(b) notebook computer

(c) Tablet PC

(d) PDA

A PDA (Personal Digital Assistant) is a lightweight mobile device that easily fits in your pocket, which makes it ideal if you require a mobile computing device as you move from place to place. PDAs provide personal organizer functions, such as a calendar, appointment book, address book, and thousands of other applications. Some PDAs also function as a cellular telephone. The small size of the processor, screen, and keyboard, however, limit a PDA's capabilities when compared with a desktop or notebook computer. For this reason, most people who purchase PDAs also have a desktop or notebook computer to handle heavy-duty applications.

Drawbacks of mobile computers and devices are that they tend to have a shorter useful lifetime than desktop computers, cost more than desktop computers, and lack the high-end capabilities. Their portability makes them susceptible to vibrations, heat or cold, and accidental drops, which can cause components such as hard disks or monitors to fail. Also, because of their size and portability, they are easy to lose and are the prime targets of thieves.

For what purposes will you use the computer?

Having a general idea of the purposes for which you want to use your computer will help you decide on the type of computer to buy. At this point in your research, it is not necessary to know the exact application software titles or version numbers you might want to use. Knowing that you plan to use the computer primarily to create word processing, spreadsheet, database, and presentation documents, however, will point you in the direction of a desktop or notebook computer. If you plan to use a mobile device to get organized, then a PDA may be your best choice. If you want the portability of a PDA, but need more computing power, then a Tablet PC may

be the best alternative. You also must consider that some application software runs only on a Mac, while others run only on a PC with the Windows operating system. Still other software may run only on a PC running the UNIX or Linux operating system.

Should the computer be compatible with the computers at school or work?

If you plan to bring work home, telecommute, or take distance education courses, then you should purchase a computer that is compatible with those at school or work. Compatibility is primarily a software issue. If your computer runs the same operating system version, such as Windows XP, and the same application software, such as Office XP, then your computer will be able to read documents created at school or work and vice versa. Incompatible hardware can become an issue if you plan to connect directly to a school or office network using a cable or wireless technology. You usually can obtain the minimum system requirements from the Information Technology department at your school or workplace.

Should the computer be a Mac or PC?

If you ask a friend, coworker, or instructor, which is better — a Mac or a PC — you may be surprised by the strong opinion expressed in the response. No other topic in the computer industry causes more heated debate. The Mac has strengths, especially in the areas of graphics, movies, photos, and music. The PC, however, has become the industry standard with 95 percent of the market share. Figure 36 compares features of the Mac and PC in several different areas. Overall, the Mac and PC have more similarities than differences, and you should consider cost, compatibility, and other factors when choosing whether to purchase a Mac or PC.

FIGURE 36 Comparison of Mac and PC features.

Area	Comparison
Cost and availability	A Mac has slightly higher prices than a PC. Mac peripherals also are more expensive. The PC offers more available models from a wide range of vendors. You can custom build, upgrade, and expand a PC for less money than a Mac.
Exterior design	The Mac has a more distinct and stylish appearance than most PCs.
Free software	Although free software for the Mac is available on the Internet, significantly more free software applications are available for the PC.
Market share	The PC dominates the personal computer market. While the Mac sells well in education, publishing, Web design, graphics, and music, the PC is the overwhelming favorite of businesses.
Operating system	Both Mac OS X and Windows XP are stable. Users claim that Mac OS X provides a better all-around user experience than Windows XP. The PC supports other operating systems, such as Linux and UNIX.
Program control	Both have simple and intuitive graphical user interfaces. The Mac relies more on the mouse and less on keyboard shortcuts than the PC. The mouse on the Mac has one button, whereas the mouse on a PC has a minimum of two buttons.
Software availability	The basic application software most users require, such as the Office suite, is available for both the Mac and PC. More specialized software, however, often is only available for PCs. Many programs are released for PCs long before they are released for Macs.
Speed	The PC has faster processors to choose from than the Mac.
Viruses	Dramatically fewer viruses attack Macs. Mac viruses also generally are less infectious than PC viruses.

After evaluating the answers to these four questions, you should have a general idea of how you plan to use your computer and the type of computer you want to buy. Once you have decided on the type of computer you want, you can follow the guidelines presented in this Buyer's Guide to help you purchase a specific computer of that type, along with software, peripherals, and other accessories.

This first set of guidelines will help you purchase, install, and maintain a desktop computer. Many of the guidelines presented also apply to the purchase of a mobile computer or device, such as a notebook computer, Tablet PC, and PDA. Later in this special feature, sections on purchasing a notebook computer, PDA, or Tablet PC address additional considerations specific to those computer types.

HOW TO PURCHASE A DESKTOP COMPUTER

Once you have decided that a desktop computer is most suited to your computing needs, the next step is to determine specific software, hardware, peripheral devices, and services to purchase, as well as where to buy the computer.

Determine the specific software you want to use on your computer.

Before deciding to purchase a particular program, be sure it contains the features necessary for the tasks you want to perform. Rely on the computer users in whom you have confidence to help you decide on the software to use. The minimum requirements of the application software you select may determine the operating system (Windows XP, Linux, UNIX, Mac OS X) you need. If you have decided to use a particular operating system that does not support application software you want to use, you may be able to purchase the similar application software from other manufacturers.

Many Web sites and trade magazines, such as those listed in Figure 37, provide reviews of software products. These Web sites frequently have articles that rate computers and software on cost, performance, and support.

Your hardware requirements depend on the minimum requirements of the application software you will run on your computer. Some application software requires more memory and disk space than others, as well as additional input, output, and storage devices. For example, suppose you want to run software that can copy one CD's or DVD's contents directly to another CD or DVD, without first copying the data to your hard disk. To support that, you should consider a desktop computer or a high-end notebook computer, because the computer will need two CD or DVD drives: one that reads from a CD or DVD, and one that reads from and writes on a CD or DVD. If you plan to run software that allows your computer to work as an entertainment system, then you will need a CD or DVD drive, quality speakers, and an upgraded sound card.

Look for bundled software.

When you purchase a computer, it may come bundled with several programs. Some sellers even let you choose which application software you want. Remember, however, that bundled software has value only if you would have purchased the software even if it had not come with the computer. At the very least, you probably will want word processing software and a browser to access the Internet. If you need additional applications, such as a spreadsheet, a database, or presentation graphics, consider purchasing a software suite, such as Microsoft Works, Microsoft Office, or Sun StarOffice™, which include several programs at a reduced price.

FIGURE 37 Hardware and software reviews.

Type of Computers	Web Site	URL
PC	Computer Shopper	shopper.cnet.com
	PC World Magazine	pcworld.com
	BYTE Magazine	byte.com
	PC Magazine	zdnet.com/reviews
	Yahoo! Computers	computers.yahoo.com
	Microsoft Network	eshop.msn.com
	Dave's Guide to Buying a Home Computer	css.msu.edu/PC-Guide
Mac	ZDNet News	zdnet.com/mac
	Macworld Magazine	macworld.com
	Apple	apple.com
	Switch to Mac Campaign	apple.com/switch

For an updated list of hardware and software reviews and their Web site addresses, visit scsite.com/dc2004/ch8/buyers.

3 Avoid buying the least powerful computer available.

Once you know the application software you want to use, you then can consider the following important criteria about the computer's components: (1) processor speed, (2) size and types of memory (RAM) and storage, (3) types of input/output devices, (4) types of ports and adapter cards, and (5) types of communications devices. The information in Figure 38 and Figure 39 (on page COM-24) can help you determine what system components are best for you. Figure 38 outlines considerations for specific hardware components. Figure 39 provides a Base Components worksheet that lists PC recommendations for each category of user discussed in this book: Home User, Small Office/Home Office User, Mobile User, Large Business User, and Power User. In the worksheet, the Home User category is divided into two groups: Application Home User and Game Home User. The Mobile User recommendations list criteria for a notebook computer, but do not include the PDA or Tablet PC options.

Computer technology changes rapidly, meaning a computer that seems powerful enough today may not serve your computing needs in a few years. In fact, studies show that many users regret not buying a more powerful computer. To avoid this, plan to buy a computer that will last you for two to three years. You can help delay obsolescence by purchasing the fastest processor, the most memory, and the largest hard disk you can afford. If you must buy a less powerful computer, be sure you can upgrade it with additional memory, components, and peripheral devices as your computer requirements grow.

FIGURE 38 Hardware guidelines.

CD/DVD Drives: Most computers come with a 32X to 48X speed CD-ROM drive that can read CDs. If you plan to write music, audio files, and documents on a CD or DVD, then you should consider upgrading to a CD-RW. An even better alternative is to upgrade to a DVD+RW/CD-RW combination drive. It allows you to read DVDs and CDs and to write data on (burn) a DVD or CD. A DVD has a capacity of at least 4.7 GB versus the 650 MB capacity of a CD.

Card Reader: A card reader is useful for transferring data directly from a removable flash memory card, such as the ones used in your camera or music player. Make sure the card reader can read the flash memory cards that you use.

Digital Camera: Consider an inexpensive point-and-shoot digital camera. They are small enough to carry around, usually operate automatically in terms of lighting and focus, and contain storage cards for storing photographs. A 1.3- to 2.2-megapixel camera with an 8 MB or 16 MB storage card is fine for creating images for use on the Web or to send via e-mail.

Digital Video Capture Device: A digital video capture device allows you to connect your computer to a camcorder or VCR and record, edit, manage, and then write video back to a VCR tape, a CD, or a DVD. The digital video capture device can be an external device or an adapter card. To create quality video (true 30 frames per second, full-sized TV), the digital video capture device should have a USB 2.0 or FireWire port. You will find that a standard USB port is too slow to maintain video quality. You also will need sufficient storage: an hour of data on a VCR tape takes up about 5 GB of disk storage.

Floppy Disk Drive: Make sure the computer you purchase has a standard 3.5", 1.44 MB floppy disk drive. A floppy disk drive is useful for backing up and transferring files.

Hard Disk: It is recommended that you buy a computer with 40 to 60 GB if your primary interests are browsing the Web and using e-mail and Office suite-type applications; 60 to 80 GB if you also want to edit digital photographs; 80 to 100 GB if you plan to edit digital video or manipulate large audio files even occasionally; and 100 to 160 GB if you will edit digital video, movies, or photography often or store audio files and music or consider yourself to be a power user.

Joystick/Wheel: If you use your computer to play games, then you will want to purchase a joystick or a wheel. These devices, especially the more expensive ones, provide for realistic game play with force feedback, programmable buttons, and specialized levers and wheels.

Keyboard: The keyboard is one of the more important devices used to communicate with the computer. For this reason, make sure the keyboard you purchase has 101 to 105 keys, is comfortable, easy to use, and has a USB connection. A wireless keyboard should be considered, especially if you have a small desk area.

Microphone: If you plan to record audio or use speech recognition to enter text and commands, then purchase a close-talk headset with gain adjustment support.

Modem: Most computers come with a modem so that you can use your telephone line to dial out and access the Internet. Some modems also have fax capabilities. Your modem should be rated at 56 Kbps.

Monitor: The monitor is where you will view documents, read e-mail messages, and view pictures. A minimum of a 17" screen is recommended, but if you are planning to use your computer for graphic design or game playing, then you may want to purchase a 19" or 21" monitor. The LCD flat panel monitor should be considered, especially if space is an issue.

Mouse: As you work with your computer, you use the mouse constantly. For this reason, spend a few extra dollars, if necessary, and purchase a mouse with an optical sensor and USB connection. The optical sensor replaces the need for a mouse ball, which means you do not need a mouse pad. For a PC, make sure your mouse has a wheel, which acts as a third button in addition to the top two buttons on the left and right. An ergonomic design is also important because your hand is on the mouse most of the time when you are using your computer. A wireless mouse should be considered to eliminate the cord and allow you to work at short distances from your computer.

Network Card: If you plan to connect to a network or use broadband (cable or DSL) to connect to the Internet, then you will need to purchase a network card. Broadband connections require a 10/100 PCI Ethernet network card.

Printer: Your two basic printer choices are ink-jet and laser. Color ink-jet printers cost on average between $50 and $300. Laser printers cost from $300 to $2,000. In general, the cheaper the printer, the lower the resolution and speed, and the more often you are required to change the ink cartridge or toner. Laser printers print faster and with a higher quality than an ink-jet, and their toner on average costs less. If you want color, then go with a high-end ink-jet printer to ensure quality of print. Duty cycle (the number of pages you expect to print each month) also should be a determining factor. If your duty cycle is on the low end — hundreds of pages per month — then stay with a high-end ink-jet printer, rather than purchasing a laser printer. If you plan to print photographs taken with a digital camera, then you should purchase a photo printer. A photo printer is a dye-sublimation printer or an ink-jet printer with higher resolution and features that allow you to print quality photographs.

Processor: For a PC, a 2.0 GHz Intel or AMD processor is more than enough processor power for application home and small office/home office users. Game home, large business, and power users should upgrade to faster processors.

RAM: RAM plays a vital role in the speed of your computer. Make sure the computer you purchase has at least 256 MB of RAM. If you have extra money to invest in your computer, then consider increasing the RAM to 512 MB or more. The extra money for RAM will be well spent.

Scanner: The most popular scanner purchased with a computer today is the flatbed scanner. When evaluating a flatbed scanner, check the color depth and resolution. Do not buy anything less than a color depth of 48 bits and a resolution of 1200 x 2400 dpi. The higher the color depth, the more accurate the color. A higher resolution picks up the more subtle gradations of color.

Sound Card: Most sound cards today support the Sound Blaster and General MIDI standards and should be capable of recording and playing digital audio. If you plan to turn your computer into an entertainment system or are a game home user, then you will want to spend the extra money and upgrade from the standard sound card.

Speakers: Once you have a good sound card, quality speakers and a separate subwoofer that amplifies the bass frequencies of the speakers can turn your computer into a premium stereo system.

Video Graphics Card: Most standard video cards satisfy the monitor display needs of application home and small office users. If you are a game home user or a graphic designer, you will want to upgrade to a higher quality video card. The higher refresh rates will further enhance the display of games, graphics, and movies.

PC Video Camera: A PC video camera is a small camera used to capture and display live video (in some cases with sound), primarily on a Web page. You also can capture, edit, and share video and still photos. The camera sits on your monitor or desk. Recommended minimum specifications include 640 x 480 resolution, a video with a rate of 30 frames per second, and a USB 2.0 or FireWire connection.

Wireless LAN Access Point: A Wireless LAN Access Point allows you to network several computers, so they can share files and access the Internet through a single cable modem or DSL connection. Each device that you connect requires a wireless card. A Wireless LAN Access Point can offer a range of operation to several hundred feet, so be sure the device has a high-powered antenna.

Zip® Drive: Consider purchasing a Zip® or Peerless® disk drive to back up important files. The Zip® drive, which has a capacity of up to 750 MB, is sufficient for most users. An alternative to purchasing a backup drive is to purchase a CD-RW or DVD+RW and burn backups of key files on a CD or DVD.

Consider upgrades to the mouse, keyboard, monitor, printer, microphone, and speakers.

You use these peripheral devices to interact with your computer, so you should make sure they are up to your standards. Review the peripheral devices listed in Figure 38 on the pages COM-22 and COM-23 and then visit both local computer dealers and large retail stores to test the computers on display. Ask the salesperson what input and output devices would be best for you and whether you should upgrade beyond what comes standard. A few extra dollars spent on these components when you initially purchase a computer can extend its usefulness by years.

Determine whether you want to use telephone lines or broadband (cable or DSL) to access the Internet.

If your computer has a modem, then you can access the Internet using a standard telephone line. Ordinarily, you call a local or toll-free 800 number to connect to an ISP (see Guideline 6). Using a dial-up Internet connection is relatively inexpensive, but slow.

DSL and cable connections provide much faster Internet connections, which are ideal if you want faster file download speeds for software, digital photos, and music. As you would expect, they also are more expensive. DSL, which is available through local telephone companies, also may require that you subscribe to an ISP. Cable is available through your local cable television provider and some online service providers (OSPs). If you get cable, then you would not use a separate Internet service provider or online service provider.

FIGURE 39 Base computer components and optional components. A copy of the Base Components worksheet is on the Data Disk. To obtain a copy of the Data Disk, see the inside back cover of this book for instructions.

BASE COMPONENTS

	Application Home User	Game Home User	Small Office/Home Office User	Mobile User	Large Business User	Power User
HARDWARE						
Processor	Pentium®4 at 2.0 GHz	Pentium®4 at 3.0 GHz	Pentium®4 at 2.0 GHz	Pentium®4 at 1.8 GHz	Pentium®4 at 3.0 GHz	Multiple Itanium(TM) at 2.5 GHz
RAM	256 MB	512 MB	256 MB	256 MB	512 MB	1 GB
Cache	256 KB L2	512 KB L2	512 KB L2	512 KB L2	512 KB L2	2 MB L3
Hard Disk	60 GB	120 GB	100 GB	40 GB	160 GB	160 GB
Monitor/LCD Flat Panel	17" or 19"	23"	19" or 21"	16.1" SuperVGA+ TFT	19" or 21"	23"
Video Graphics Card	64 MB	128 MB	64 MB	16 MB	64 MB	128 MB
CD/DVD Bay 1	48x CD-ROM	48x CD-ROM	48x CD-ROM	24x CD-ROM	48x CD-ROM	48x CD-ROM
CD/DVD Bay 2	32x/10x/40x CD-RW/DVD	DVD+RW/CD-RW	32x/10x/40x CD-RW/DVD	24x CD-RW/DVD	DVD+RW/CD-RW	DVD+RW/CD-RW
Floppy Disk Drive	3.5"	3.5"	3.5"	3.5"	3.5"	3.5"
Printer	Color Ink-Jet	Color Ink-Jet	10 ppm Laser	Portable Ink-Jet	24 ppm Laser	10 ppm Laser
PC Video Camera	Yes	Yes	Yes	Yes	Yes	Yes
Fax/Modem	Yes	Yes	Yes	Yes	Yes	Yes
Microphone	Close-Talk Headset with Gain Adjustment	Close-Talk Headset with Gain Adjustment	Close-Talk Headset with Gain Adjustment	Close-Talk Headset with Gain Adjustment	Close-Talk Headset with Gain Adjustment	Close-Talk Headset with Gain Adjustment
Speakers	Stereo	Full-Dolby Surround	Stereo	Stereo	Stereo	Full-Dolby
Pointing Device	IntelliMouse or Optical Mouse	Optical Mouse and Joystick	IntelliMouse or Optical Mouse	Touchpad or Pointing Stick and Optical Mouse	IntelliMouse or Optical Mouse	IntelliMouse or Optical Mouse and Joystick
Keyboard	Yes	Yes	Yes	Built-In	Yes	Yes
Backup Disk/Tape Drive	750 MB Zip®	10 GB Peerless™	10 GB Peerless™	10 GB Peerless™	20 GB Peerless™	20 GB Peerless™
Sound Card	Sound Blaster Compatible	Sound Blaster Compatible	Sound Blaster Compatible	Built-In	Sound Blaster Compatible	Sound Blaster
Network Card	Yes	Yes	Yes	Yes	Yes	Yes
TV-Out Connector	Yes	Yes	Yes	Yes	Yes	Yes
USB Port	Yes	Yes	Yes	Yes	Yes	Yes
FireWire Port	Yes	Yes	Yes	Yes	Yes	Yes
SOFTWARE						
Operating System	Windows XP Home Edition	Windows XP Home Edition	Windows XP Professional	Windows XP Professional	Windows XP Professional	Windows XP Professional
Application Suite	Office XP Standard Edition	Office XP Standard Edition	Office XP Small Business Edition	Office XP Small Business Edition	Office XP Professional with FrontPage 2002	Office XP Professional with FrontPage 2002
AntiVirus	Yes, 12-Mo. Subscription	Yes, 12-Mo. Subscription	Yes, 12-Mo. Subscription	Yes, 12-Mo. Subscription	Yes, 12-Mo. Subscription	Yes, 12-Mo. Subscription
Internet Access	Cable, DSL, or Dial-up	Cable, DSL, or Dial-up	Cable, DSL, or Dial-up	Satellite or Cellular	LAN/WAN (T1/T3)	Cable or DSL
OTHER						
Surge Protector	Yes	Yes	Yes	Portable	Yes	Yes
Warranty	3-Year Limited, 1-Year Next Business Day On-Site Service	3-Year Limited, 1-Year Next Business Day On-Site Service	3-year On-Site Service	3-Year Limited, 1-Year Next Business Day On-Site Service	3-year On-Site Service	3-year On-Site Service
Other		Wheel	Postage Printer	Docking Station Carrying Case Fingerprint Scanner Portable Data Projector		Graphics Tablet Plotter or Large-Format Printer

Optional Components for all Categories

802.11b Wireless Card	Graphics Tablet
Bluetooth™ Enabled	iPod Music Player
Biometric Input Device	IrDa Port
Card Reader	Mouse Pad/Wrist Rest
Digital Camera	Multifunction Peripheral
Digital Video Capture	Photo Printer
Digital Video Camera	Portable Data Projector
Dual-Monitor Support with Second Monitor	Scanner
Ergonomic Keyboard	TV/FM Tuner
External Hard Disk	Uninterruptible Power Supply
	USB Drive

6 If you are using a dial-up or wireless connection to connect to the Internet, then select an ISP or OSP.

You can access the Internet via telephone lines in one of two ways: via an ISP or an OSP. Both provide Internet access for a monthly fee that ranges from $6 to $25. If you are using DSL, you will have to pay additional costs for a residential DSL line. Local ISPs offer Internet access to users in a limited geographic region, through local telephone numbers. National ISPs provide access for users nationwide (including mobile users), through local and toll-free telephone numbers and cable. Because of their size, national ISPs generally offer more services and have a larger technical support staff than local ISPs. OSPs furnish Internet access as well as members-only features for users nationwide. Figure 40 lists several national ISPs and OSPs. Before you choose an ISP or OSP, compare such features as the number of access hours, monthly fees, available services (e-mail, Web page hosting, chat), and reliability.

7 Use a worksheet to compare computers, services, and other considerations.

You can use a separate sheet of paper to take notes on each vendor's computer and then summarize the information on a worksheet, such as the one shown in Figure 41. You can use Figure 41 to compare prices for either a PC or a MAC. Most companies advertise a price for a base computer that includes components housed in the system unit (processor, RAM, sound card, video card), disk drives (floppy disk, hard disk, CD-ROM, CD-RW, DVD-ROM, and DVD+RW), a keyboard, mouse, monitor, printer, speakers, and modem. Be aware, however, that some advertisements list prices for computers with only some of these components.

Monitors and printers, for example, often are not included in a base computer's price. Depending on how you plan to use the computer, you may want to invest in additional or more powerful components. When you are comparing the prices of computers, make sure you are comparing identical or similar configurations.

 8 If you are buying a new computer, you have several purchasing options: buying from your school bookstore, a local computer dealer, a local large retail store, or ordering by mail via telephone or the Web.

Each purchasing option has certain advantages. Many college bookstores, for example, sign exclusive pricing agreements with computer manufacturers and, thus, can offer student discounts. Local dealers and local large retail stores, however, more easily can provide hands-on support. Mail-order companies that sell computers by telephone or online via the Web (Figure 42 on the next page) often provide the lowest prices, but extend less personal service. Some major mail-order companies, however, have started to provide next-business-day, on-site services. A credit card usually is required to buy from a mail-order company. Figure 43 on the next page lists some of the more popular mail-order companies and their Web site addresses.

FIGURE 41 A worksheet is an effective tool for summarizing and comparing the prices and components of different computer vendors. A copy of the Computer Cost Comparison Worksheet for the PC or Mac is on the Data Disk. To obtain a copy of the Data Disk, see the inside back cover of this book for instructions.

FIGURE 40 National ISPs and OSPs.

Company	Service	URL
America Online	OSP	aol.com
AT&T WorldNet	ISP	www.att.net
CompuServe	OSP	compuserve.com
EarthLink®	ISP	earthlink.net
Juno®	OSP	juno.com
NetZero®	OSP	netzero.com
Prodigy™	ISP/OSP	www.prodigy.net
MSN	OSP	msn.com

For an updated list of national ISPs and OSPs and their Web site addresses, visit scsite.com/dc2004/ch8/buyers.

PC or MAC Cost Comparison Worksheet

Dealers list prices for computers with most of these components (instead of listing individual component costs). Some dealers do not supply a monitor. Some dealers offer significant discounts, but you must subscribe to an Internet service for a specified period to receive the discounted price. To compare computers, enter overall system price at top and enter a 0 (zero) for components included in the system cost. For any additional components not covered in the system price, enter the cost in the appropriate cells.

Items to Purchase	Desired System (PC)	Desired System (Mac)	Local Dealer #1	Local Dealer #2	Online Dealer #1	Online Dealer #2	Comments
			Prices				
OVERALL SYSTEM							
Overall System Price	< $1,500	< $1,500					
HARDWARE							
Processor	Pentium® 4 at 2.0 GHz	PowerPC G4 at 800 MHz					
RAM	256 MB	256 MB					
Cache	256 KB L2	256 KB L2					
Hard Disk	80 GB	80 GB					
Monitor	17 Inch	17 Inch					
Video Graphics Card	64 MB	64 MB					
Floppy Disk Drive	3.5 Inch	3.5 Inch					
CD/DVD Bay 1	48x CD-ROM	32x/10x/40x CD-RW/DVD					
CD/DVD Bay 2	32x/10x/40x CD-RW/DVD	NA					
Speakers	Stereo	Stereo					
Sound Card	Sound Blaster Compatible	Sound Blaster Compatible					
USB Ports	2	2					
FireWire Port	2	2					
Network Card	Yes	Yes					
Fax/Modem	56 Kbps	56 Kbps					
Keyboard	Standard	Apple Pro Keyboard Intellimouse or					
Pointing Device	IntelliMouse	Apple Pro Mouse					
Microphone	Close-Talk Headset with Gain Adjustment	Close-Talk Headset with Gain Adjustment					
Printer	Color Ink-Jet	Color Ink-Jet					
Printer Cable	Yes	Yes					
Backup	250 MB Zip®	250 MB Zip®					
SOFTWARE							
Operating System	Windows XP Home Edition	Mac OS X					
Application Software	Office XP Small Business Edition	Office v.X for Mac					
Antivirus	Yes - 12 Mo. Subscription	Yes - 12 Mo. Subscription					
OTHER							
Card Reader	MemoryStick Dual	MemoryStick Dual					
Digital Camera	2-Megapixel	2-Megapixel					
Internet Connection	1-Year Subscription	1-Year Subscription					
Joystick	Yes	Yes					
PC Video Camera	With Microphone	With Microphone					
Scanner							
Surge Protector							
Warranty	3-Year On-Site Service	3-Year On-Site Service					
Wireless card	Internal	Internal					
Wireless LAN Access Point	LinkSys	Apple AirPort					
Total Cost			$.	$.	$.	$.	

If you are buying a used computer, stay with name brands such as Dell, Gateway, Hewlett-Packard, and Apple.

Although brand-name equipment can cost more, most brand-name computers have longer, more comprehensive warranties, are better supported, and have more authorized centers for repair services. As with new computers, you can purchase a used computer from local computer dealers, local large retail stores, or mail order via the telephone or the Web. Classified ads and used computer sellers offer additional outlets for purchasing used computers. Figure 44 lists several major used computer brokers and their Web site addresses.

 If you have a computer and are upgrading to a new one, then consider selling or trading in the old one.

If you are a replacement buyer, your older computer still may have value. If you cannot sell the computer through the classified ads, via a Web site, or to a friend, then ask if the computer dealer will buy your old computer. An increasing number of companies are taking trade-ins, but do not expect too much money for your old computer.

 Be aware of hidden costs.

Before purchasing, be sure to consider any additional costs associated with buying a computer, such as an additional telephone line, a cable or DSL modem, an uninterruptible power supply (UPS), computer furniture, floppy disks and paper, and computer training classes you may want to take. Depending on where you buy your computer, the seller may be willing to include some or all of these in the computer purchase price.

 Consider more than just price.

The lowest-cost computer may not be the best long-term buy. Consider such intangibles as the vendor's time in business, the vendor's regard for quality, and the vendor's reputation for support. If you need to upgrade your computer often, you may want to consider a leasing arrangement, in which you pay monthly lease fees, but can upgrade or add on to your computer as your equipment needs change. No matter what type of buyer you are, insist on a 30-day, no-questions-asked return policy on your computer.

FIGURE 43 New computer mail-order companies.

Type of Computer	Company	URL
PC	Computer Shopper	shopper.cnet.com
	HP/Compaq	thenew.hp.com
	CompUSA	compusa.com
	dartek.com™	dartek.com
	Dell	dell.com
	Gateway	gateway.com
	Micron	micron.com
Macintosh	Apple Computer	store.apple.com
	Club Mac	clubmac.com
	MacConnection	macconnection.com
	MacExchange	macx.com

For an updated list of new computer mail-order companies and their Web site addresses, visit scsite.com/dc2004/ch8/buyers.

FIGURE 42 Mail-order companies, such as Dell, sell computers online.

FIGURE 44 Used computer mail-order companies.

Company	URL
Amazon.com	amazon.com
Off Lease Computer Supermarket	off-leasecomputers.com
American Computer Exchange	www.amcoex.com
U.S. Computer Exchange	uscomputerexchange.com
eBay	ebay.com

For an updated list of used computer mail-order companies and their Web site addresses, visit scsite.com/dc2004/ch8/buyers.

13 Avoid restocking fees.

Some companies charge a restocking fee of 10 to 20 percent as part of their money-back return policy. In some cases, no restocking fee for hardware is applied, but it is applied for software. Ask about the existence and terms of any restocking policies before you buy.

14 Consider purchasing an extended warranty or service plan.

If you use your computer for business or require fast resolution to major computer problems, consider purchasing an extended warranty or a service plan through a local dealer or third-party company. Most extended warranties cover the repair and replacement of computer components beyond the standard warranty. Most service plans ensure that your technical support calls receive priority response from technicians. You also can purchase an on-site service plan that states that a technician will come to your home, work, or school within 24 hours. If your computer includes a warranty and service agreement for a year or less, think about extending the service for two or three years when you buy the computer.

15 Use a credit card to purchase your new computer.

Many credit cards offer purchase protection and extended warranty benefits that cover you in case of loss of or damage to purchased goods. Paying by credit card also gives you time to install and use the computer before you have to pay for it. Finally, if you are dissatisfied with the computer and are unable to reach an agreement with the seller, paying by credit card gives you certain rights regarding withholding payment until the dispute is resolved. Check your credit card terms for specific details.

HOW TO PURCHASE A NOTEBOOK COMPUTER

If you need computing capability when you travel or to use in lecture or meetings, you may find a notebook computer to be an appropriate choice. The guidelines mentioned in the previous section also apply to the purchase of a notebook computer. The following are additional considerations unique to notebook computers.

1 Purchase a notebook computer with a sufficiently large active-matrix screen.

Active-matrix screens display high-quality color that is viewable from all angles. Less expensive, passive-matrix screens sometimes are difficult to see in low-light conditions and cannot be viewed from an angle. Notebook computers typically come with a 12.1-inch, 13.3-inch, 14.1-inch, 15-inch, or 16.1-inch display. For most users, a 14.1-inch display is satisfactory. If you intend to use your notebook computer as a desktop computer replacement, however, you may opt for a 15-inch or 16.1-inch display. Notebook computers with these larger displays weigh seven to ten pounds, however, so if you travel a lot and portability is essential, you might want a lighter computer with a smaller display. The lightest notebook computers, which weigh less than 3 pounds, are equipped with a 12.1-inch display. Regardless of size, the resolution of the display should be at least 1024 x 768 pixels. To compare the monitor size on various notebook computers, visit the company Web sites in Figure 45.

FIGURE 45 Companies that sell notebook computers.

Type of Notebook	Company	URL
PC	Acer	acer.com
	Dell	dell.com
	Fujitsu	fujitsu.com
	Gateway	gateway.com
	HP	hp.com
	IBM	ibm.com
	NEC	nec.com
	Sony	sony.com
	Sharp	sharp.com
	Toshiba	toshiba.com
Mac	Apple	apple.com

For an updated list of companies and their Web site addresses, visit scsite.com/dc2004/ch8/buyers.

Experiment with different keyboards and pointing devices.

Notebook computer keyboards are far less standardized than those for desktop computers. Some notebook computers, for example, have wide wrist rests, while others have none. Notebook computers also use a range of pointing devices, including pointing sticks, touchpads, and trackballs. Before you purchase a notebook computer, try various types of keyboard and pointing devices to determine which is easiest for you to use. Regardless of the pointing device you select, you also may want to purchase a regular mouse to use when you are working at a desk or other large surface.

Make sure the notebook computer you purchase has a CD and/or DVD drive.

Loading and installing software, especially large Office suites, is much faster if done from a CD-ROM, CD-RW, DVD-ROM, or DVD+RW. Today, most notebook computers come with an internal or external CD-ROM drive. Some notebook computers even come with a CD-ROM drive and a CD-RW drive or a DVD-ROM drive and a CD-RW or DVD+RW/CD-RW drive. Although DVD drives are more expensive, they allow you to play CDs and DVD movies using your notebook computer and a headset.

If necessary, upgrade the processor, memory, and disk storage at the time of purchase.

As with a desktop computer, upgrading your notebook computer's memory and disk storage usually is less expensive at the time of initial purchase. Some disk storage is custom designed for notebook computer manufacturers, meaning an upgrade might not be available in the future. If you are purchasing a lightweight notebook computer, then it should include at least a 1.4 GHz processor, 256 MB RAM, and 40 GB of storage.

The availability of built-in ports on a notebook computer is important.

A notebook computer does not have a lot of room to add adapter cards. If you know the purpose for which you plan to use your notebook computer, then you can determine the ports you will need. Most notebooks come with common ports, such as a mouse port, IrDA port, serial port, parallel port, video port, and USB port. If you plan to connect your notebook computer to a TV, however, then you will need a PC-to-TV port. If you want to connect to networks at school or in various offices, make sure the notebook computer you purchase has a built-in network card. If your notebook computer does not come with a network card built-in, then you will have to purchase an external network card that slides into an expansion slot in your notebook computer, as well as a network cable. If you expect to connect an iPod portable digital music player to your notebook computer, then you will need a FireWire port.

If you plan to use your notebook computer for note-taking at school or in meetings, consider a notebook computer that converts to a Tablet PC.

Some computer manufacturers have developed convertible notebook computers that allow the screen to rotate 180 degrees on a central hinge and then fold down to cover the keyboard and become a Tablet PC (Figure 46). You then can use a pencil-like device to input text or drawings into the computer by writing on the screen.

Consider purchasing a notebook computer with a built-in wireless card to connect to your home network.

Many users today are setting up wireless home networks. With a wireless home network, the desktop computer functions as the server and your notebook computer can access the desktop computer from any location in the house to share files and hardware, such as a printer, and browse the Web. If your notebook computer does not come with a built-in wireless card, you can purchase an external one that slides into your notebook computer. Most home wireless networks allow connections from distances of 150 to 800 feet.

FIGURE 46 The Acer TravelMate 100 notebook computer converts to a Tablet PC.

If you are going to use your notebook computer for long periods without access to an electrical outlet, purchase a second battery.

The trend among notebook computer users today is power and size over battery life, and notebook computer manufacturers have picked up on this. Many notebook computer users today are willing to give up longer battery life for a larger screen, faster processor, and bigger storage. For this reason, you need to be careful in choosing a notebook computer if you plan to use it without access to electrical outlets for long periods, such as an airplane flight. You also might want to purchase a second battery as a backup. If you anticipate running your notebook computer on batteries frequently, choose a computer that uses lithium-ion batteries (they last longer than nickel cadmium or nickel hydride batteries).

 Purchase a well-padded and well-designed carrying case.

An amply padded carrying case will protect your notebook computer from the bumps it will receive while traveling. A well-designed carrying case will have room for accessories such as spare floppy disks, CDs and DVDs, a user manual, pens, and paperwork (Figure 47).

 If you travel overseas, obtain a set of electrical and telephone adapters.

Different countries use different outlets for electrical and telephone connections. Several manufacturers sell sets of adapters that will work in most countries (Figure 48).

 If you plan to connect your notebook computer to a video projector, make sure the notebook computer is compatible with the video projector.

You should check, for example, to be sure that your notebook computer will allow you to display an image on the computer screen and projection device at the same time (Figure 49). Also, ensure that your notebook computer has the ports required to connect to the video projector.

 For improved security, consider a fingerprint scanner.

More than a quarter million notebook computers are stolen or lost each year. If you have critical information stored on your notebook computer, then consider purchasing one with a fingerprint scanner to protect the data if your computer is stolen or lost. Fingerprint security offers a level of protection that extends well beyond the standard password protection.

FIGURE 48 Set of electrical and telephone adapters for travel abroad.

FIGURE 47 Well-designed carrying case.

FIGURE 49 A notebook computer connected to a video projector to project what displays on the screen.

HOW TO PURCHASE A TABLET PC

The Tablet PC (Figure 50) combines the mobility features of a traditional notebook computer with the simplicity of pencil and paper, because you can create and save Office-type documents by writing and drawing directly on the screen with a digital pen. Tablet PCs use the Windows XP Tablet PC Edition operating system, which expands on Windows XP Professional by including digital pen and speech capabilities. A notebook computer and a Tablet PC have many similarities. For this reason, if you are considering purchasing a Tablet PC, review the guidelines for purchasing a notebook computer, as well as the guidelines below.

 Make sure the Tablet PC fits your mobile computing needs.

The Tablet PC is not for every mobile user. If you find yourself in need of a computer in class or you are spending more time in meetings than in your office, then the Tablet PC may be the answer. Before you invest money in a Tablet PC, however, determine the programs you plan to use it for. You should not buy a Tablet PC simply because it is a new and interesting type of computer. For additional information about the Tablet PC, visit the Web sites listed in Figure 51. You may have to use the search capabilities on the home page of the companies listed to locate information about the Tablet PC.

Decide whether you want a convertible or pure Tablet PC.

Convertible Tablet PCs have an attached keyboard and look like a notebook computer. You rotate the screen and lay it flat against the computer for note-taking. The pure Tablet PCs are slim and lightweight, weighing less than four pounds. They have the capability of easily docking at a desktop to gain access to a large monitor, keyboard, and mouse. If you spend a lot of time attending lectures or meetings, than the pure Tablet PC is ideal. Acceptable specifications for a Tablet PC are shown in Figure 52.

FIGURE 51 Companies involved with Tablet PCs and their Web sites.

Company	URL
Acer	acer.com/us
Fujitsu	fujitsu.com
Hewlett-Packard	hp.com
Microsoft	microsoft.com/windowsxp/tabletpc
ViewSonic	viewsonic.com
VIA Technologies	via.com

For an updated list of companies and their Web site addresses, visit scsite.com/dc2004/ch8/buyers.

FIGURE 52 Tablet PC specifications.

Tablet PC Specifications	
Dimensions	12" x 9" x 1.5"
Weight	Less than 4 Pounds
Processor	Pentium III at 2.0 GHz
RAM	128 MB
Hard Disk	20 GB
Display	10.4" XGA TFT 16-Bit Color
Digitizer	Electromagnetic Digitizer
Battery	4-Cell (3-Hour)
USB	2
FireWire	1
Docking Station	Grab and Go with CD-ROM, Keyboard, and Mouse
Bluetooth Port	Yes
802.11b Card	Yes
Network Card	10/100 Ethernet
Modem	56 Kbps
Speakers	Internal
Microphone	Internal
Operating System	Windows XP Tablet PC Edition
Application Software	Office XP Small Business Edition
Antivirus Software	Yes - 12 Month Subscription
Warranty	1-Year Limited Warranty Parts and Labor

FIGURE 50 The lightweight Tablet PC, with its handwriting capabilities, is the latest addition to the family of mobile computers.

Be sure the weight and dimensions are conducive to portability.

The weight and dimensions of the Tablet PC are important because you carry it around like a notepad. The Tablet PC you buy should weigh in at four pounds or less. Its dimensions should be approximately 12 inches by 9 inches by 1.5 inches.

 Port availability, battery life, and durability are even more important with a Tablet PC than they are with a notebook computer.

Make sure the Tablet PC you purchase has the ports required for the applications you plan to run. As with any mobile computer, battery life is important, especially if you plan to use your Tablet PC for long periods without access to an electrical outlet. A Tablet PC must be durable because if you use it for what it was built for, then you will be handling it much like you handle a pad of paper.

Experiment with different models of the Tablet PC to find the digital pen that works best for you.

The key to making use of the Tablet PC is to be comfortable with its handwriting capabilities and on-screen keyboard. Not only is the digital pen used to write on the screen (Figure 53), but you also use it to make gestures to complete tasks, in a manner similar to the way you use a mouse. Figure 54 compares the standard point-and-click of a mouse unit with the gestures made with a digital pen. Other gestures with the digital pen replicate some of the commonly used keys on a keyboard.

 Check out the comfort level of handwriting in different positions.

You should be able to handwrite on a Tablet PC with your hand resting on the screen. You also should be able to handwrite holding the Tablet PC in one hand, as well as with it sitting in your lap.

FIGURE 53 A Tablet PC lets you handwrite notes and draw on the screen using a digital pen.

 Make sure the LCD display device has a resolution high enough to take advantage of Microsoft's ClearType technologies.

Tablet PCs use a digitizer under a standard 10.4-inch motion-sensitive LCD display to make the digital ink on the screen look like real ink on paper. The Tablet PC also uses ClearType technology that makes the characters crisper on the screen, so your notes are easier to read and cause less fatigue to the eyes. To ensure you get the maximum benefits from the new ClearType technology, make sure the LCD display has a resolution of 800 x 600 in landscape mode and a 600 x 800 in portrait mode.

Test the built-in Tablet PC microphone and speakers.

With many application software packages recognizing human speech, such as the Microsoft Office XP, it is important that the Tablet PC's built-in microphone operates at an acceptable level. If the microphone is not to your liking, you may want to purchase a close-talk headset with your Tablet PC. Increasingly, more users are sending information as audio files, rather than relying solely on text. For this reason, you also should check the speakers on the Tablet PC to make sure they meet your standards.

Consider a Tablet PC with a built-in PC video camera.

A PC video camera adds streaming video and still photography capabilities to your Tablet PC, while still allowing you to take notes in lecture or in meetings.

FIGURE 54 Standard point-and-click of a mouse unit compared with the gestures made with a digital pen.

Mouse Unit	Digital Pen
Point	Point
Click	Tap
Double-click	Double-tap
Right-click	Tap and hold
Click and drag	Drag

10 Review the docking capabilities of the Tablet PC.

The Windows XP Tablet PC Edition operating system supports a grab-and-go form of docking, so you can pick up and take a docked Tablet PC with you, just as you would pick up a notepad on your way to a meeting. Two basic types of docking stations are available. One type of docking station (Figure 55) changes the Tablet PC into a desktop computer. It uses the Tablet PC as a monitor. The station has a CD or DVD drive, full-size keyboard, mouse, and other accessories. Another type of docking station lets you dock your PC to your desktop computer and use Windows XP Dual Monitor support. Windows XP Dual Monitor support allows you to work on one monitor, while using the Tablet PC monitor to display often-used applications, such as your calendar or address book.

11 Wireless access to the Internet and your e-mail is essential with a Tablet PC.

Make sure the Tablet PC has wireless networking, so you can access the Internet and your e-mail anytime and anywhere. Your Tablet PC also should include standard network connections, such as dial-up and Ethernet connections.

12 Review available accessories to purchase with your Tablet PC.

Tablet PC accessories include docking stations, mouse units, keyboards, security cables, additional memory and storage, protective handgrips, screen protectors, and various types of digital pens. You should review the available accessories when you purchase a Tablet PC.

HOW TO PURCHASE A PDA

If you need to stay organized when you are on the go, then a lightweight, palm-sized or pocket-sized mobile device, called a PDA, may be the right choice. PDAs typically are categorized by the operating system they run. Although several are available, the two primary operating systems are Palm OS[®] (Figure 56) or a Windows-based operating systems, such as Pocket PC 2002 (Figure 57).

This section lists guidelines you will want to consider when purchasing a PDA. You also should visit the Web sites listed in Figure 24 to gather more information about the type of PDA that best suits your computing needs.

FIGURE 56 Sony's NR70V PDA with Palm OS. The NR70V lets you take pictures with its digital camera, listen to MP3 files, display videos and images, plus keep your datebook and contact list organized.

FIGURE 55 A Tablet PC docked to create a desktop computer with the Tablet PC as the monitor.

FIGURE 57 Compaq's iPaq H3970 with Pocket PC 2002 includes Bluetooth wireless connectivity. The iPaq plays MP3 music or audio programs from the Web, as well as records and plays back voice notes or meeting notes.

Determine the programs you plan to run on your PDA.

All PDAs can handle basic organizer-type software such as a calendar, address book, and notepad. The availability of other software depends on the operating system you choose. The depth and breadth of software for the Palm OS is significant, with more than 11,000 basic programs and over 600 wireless programs. PDAs that run Windows-based operating systems, such as Pocket PC 2002, may have fewer programs available, but the operating system and application software are similar to those with which you are familiar, such as Word and Excel.

 Consider how much you want to pay.

The price of a PDA can range from $100 to $800, depending on its capabilities. In general, Palm OS devices are at the lower end of the cost spectrum and Pocket PC and other Windows-based devices are at the higher end. For the latest PDA prices, capabilities, and accessories, visit the Web sites listed in Figure 58.

 Determine whether you need wireless access to the Internet and e-mail or mobile telephone capabilities with your PDA.

Some PDAs offer wireless access to the Internet, instant messaging, and e-mail for a monthly network connection fee. To run the wireless, the functionality of the PDAs often is stripped down to conserve battery power. Some wireless PDAs, such as Handspring's Treo 270, come with a mobile telephone built-in (Figure 59). These features and services allow PDA users to access real-time information from anywhere to help make decisions while on the go.

FIGURE 58 Reviews and information about PDAs.

Web Site	URL
Compaq	compaq.com/products/handhelds
Computer Shopper	shopper.cnet.com
Handspring	handspring.com
Microsoft	pocketpc.com
Palm	palm.com
PDA Buyers Guide	pdabuyersguide.com
Sony	sonystyle.com
Wireless Developer Network	wirelessdevnet.com
For an updated list of reviews and information about PDAs and their Web site addresses, visit scsite.com/dc2004/ch8/buyers.	

 Make sure your PDA has enough memory.

Memory (RAM) is not a major issue with low-end PDAs with monochrome displays and basic organizer functions. Memory is a major issue, however, for high-end PDAs that have color displays and wireless features. Without enough memory, the performance level of your PDA will drop dramatically. If you plan to purchase a high-end PDA running the Palm OS operating system, the PDA should have at least 16 MB of RAM. If you plan to purchase a high-end PDA running the Pocket PC 2002 operating system, the PDA should have at least 48 MB of RAM.

 Practice with the touch screen, handwriting recognition, and built-in keyboard before deciding on a model.

To enter data into a PDA, you use a pen-like stylus to handwrite on the screen or a keyboard. The keyboard either is mounted on the front of the PDA or it slides out. The Handspring Treo shown in Figure 59, comes with a small, built-in keyboard that works like a mobile telephone keypad. With handwriting recognition, the PDA translates the handwriting into a computerized font. You also can use the stylus as a pointing device to select items on the screen and enter data by tapping on an on-screen keyboard. By practicing data entry before buying a PDA, you can learn if one PDA may be easier for you to use than another. You also can buy third-party software to improve a PDA's handwriting recognition.

FIGURE 59 The Handspring Treo 270 running Palm OS has a full-color display and can be used as a telephone, an organizer, or to access e-mail and the Web.

Decide whether you want a color display.

Pocket PC devices usually come with a color display that supports as many as 65,536 colors. Palm OS devices also have a color display, but the less expensive ones have a monochrome display in 4 to 16 shades of gray. Having a color display does result in greater on-screen detail, but it also requires more memory and uses more power. Resolution also influences the quality of the display.

 Compare battery life.

Any mobile device is good only if it has the power required to run. Palm OS devices with monochrome screens typically have a much longer battery life than Pocket PC devices with color screens. To help alleviate this problem, many Palm OS and Pocket PC devices have incorporated rechargeable batteries that can be recharged by placing the PDA in a cradle or connecting it to a charger.

 Even with PDAs, seriously consider the importance of ergonomics.

Will you put the PDA in your pocket, a carrying case, wear it on your belt? How does it feel in your hand? Will you use it indoors or outdoors? Many screens are unreadable outdoors. Do you need extra ruggedness, such as would be required in construction, in a plant, or a warehouse?

 Check out the accessories.

Determine which accessories you want for your PDA. PDA accessories include carrying cases, portable mini- and full-size keyboards, removable storage, modems, synchronization cradles and cables, car chargers, wireless communications, global positioning system modules, digital camera modules, expansion cards, dashboard mounts, replacement styli, and more.

 Decide whether you want additional functionality.

In general, off-the-shelf Pocket PC devices have broader functionality than Palm OS devices. For example, voice-recording capability, e-book players, MP3 players, and video players are standard on most Pocket PC devices. If you are leaning towards a Palm OS device and want these additional functions, you can purchase additional software or expansion modules to add them later.

 Determine whether synchronization of data with other PDAs or personal computers is important.

Most PDAs come with a cradle that connects to the USB or serial port on your computer so you can synchronize data on your PDA with your desktop or notebook computer. Increasingly, more PDAs are Bluetooth and/or 802.11b enabled, which gives them the capability of synchronizing wirelessly. Most PDAs today also have an infrared port that allows you to synchronize data with any device that has a similar infrared port, including desktop and notebook computers or other PDAs.

HOW TO INSTALL A COMPUTER

It is important that you spend time planning for the installation of your computer. Follow these steps to ensure your installation experience will be a pleasant one and that your work area is safe, healthy, and efficient.

 Read the installation manuals before you start to install your equipment.

Many manufacturers include separate installation manuals that contain important information with their equipment. You can save a great deal of time and frustration if you make an effort to read the manuals before starting the installation process.

Do some additional research.

To locate additional instructions or advice about installing your computer, review the computer magazines or Web sites listed in Figure 60 to search for articles about installing a computer.

Web Site	URL
Getting Started/Installation	
HelpTalk Online	www.helptalk.com
Ergonomics	
Ergonomic Computing	cobweb.creighton.edu/training/ergo.htm
HealthyComputing.com	healthycomputing.com
IBM Healthy Computing	www.pc.ibm.com/ww/healthycomputing
Apple Ergonomics	apple.com/about/ergonomics/
Healthy Choices for Computer Users	www-ehs.ucsd.edu/ergo/ergobk/vdt.htm
Video Display Terminal Health and Safety Guidelines	uhs.berkeley.edu/Facstaff/Ergonomics

For an updated list of reference materials, visit scsite.com/dc2004/ch8/buyers.

FIGURE 60 Web references on setting up and using your personal computer.

Set up your computer in a well-designed work area and remain aware of health issues as you work.

Ergonomic studies have shown that using the correct type and configuration of chair, keyboard, monitor, and work surface will help you work comfortably and efficiently, and help protect your health. For your computer work space, experts recommend an area of at least two feet by four feet. You also should set up a document holder that keeps documents at the same height and distance as your computer screen to minimize neck and eye discomfort. Finally, use non-glare light bulbs that illuminate your entire work area to reduce eyestrain. Figure 61 illustrates additional guidelines for setting up your work area. Figure 62 provides computer user health guidelines.

 Install your computer in a work space where you can control the temperature and humidity.

You should keep the computer in an area with a constant temperature between 60°F and 80°F. High temperatures and humidity can damage electronic components. Be careful when using space heaters, for example, as the hot, dry air they generate can cause disk problems.

FIGURE 61 A well-designed work area should be flexible to allow adjustments to the height and build of different individuals. Good lighting and air quality also are important considerations.

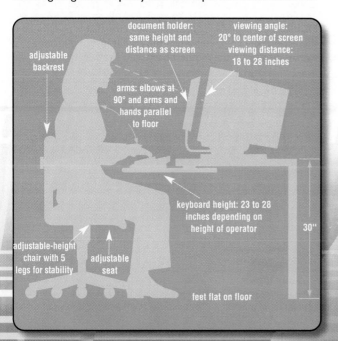

 Set up your work space near an available electrical outlet and set aside a proper location for the electrical wires.

Your computer and peripheral devices, such as the monitor and printer, require an electrical outlet. To maintain safety and simplify the connections, purchase a surge protector to connect the computer and peripheral devices to the electrical outlet. Place the electrical wires in a location where they are not a fire risk and you can avoid tripping on them. After you turn your computer off, turn the master switch on the surge protector to off.

 Have a telephone outlet and telephone or cable connection near your work space, so you can connect your modem and/or place calls while using your computer.

To plug in your modem to dial up and access the Internet, you will need a telephone outlet or cable connection close to your computer. Having a telephone nearby also helps if you need to place business or technical support calls while you are working on your computer. Often, if you call a vendor about a hardware or software problem, the support person can talk you through a correction while you are on the telephone. To avoid data loss, however, do not place floppy disks on the telephone or near any other electrical or electronic equipment.

FIGURE 62 Following these health guidelines can help computer users maintain their health.

1. Work in a well-designed work area, as shown in Figure 61.

2. Alternate work activities to prevent physical and mental fatigue. If possible, change the order of your work to provide some variety.

3. Take frequent breaks. Every 15 minutes, look away from the screen to give your eyes a break. At least once per hour, get out of your chair and move around. Every two hours, take at least a 15-minute break.

4. Incorporate hand, arm, and body stretching exercises into your breaks. During your lunch break, try to get outside and walk.

5. Make sure your computer monitor is designed to minimize electro-magnetic radiation (EMR).

6. Try to eliminate or minimize surrounding noise that contributes to stress and tension.

7. If you frequently use the telephone and the computer at the same time, consider using a telephone headset. Cradling the telephone between your head and shoulder can cause muscle strain.

8. Be aware of symptoms of repetitive strain injuries: soreness, pain, numbness, or weakness in neck, shoulders, arms, wrists, and hands. Do not ignore early signs; seek medical advice.

If you plan to set up a wireless network, choose an area that is free from potential signal interference.

Low-level basement areas, doors, trees, and walls, for example, can affect the signals between wireless devices. The signal pattern for most wireless antenna is circular, with the strongest signal closest to the antenna. The best advice is to give the antenna ample room and determine its placement by trial and error.

 Install bookshelves.

When you set up your work space, install bookshelves above and/or to the side of your computer area to keep manuals and other reference materials handy.

 Obtain a computer tool set.

Computer tool sets include any screwdrivers and other tools you might need to work on your computer. Computer dealers, office supply stores, and mail-order companies sell these tool sets. To keep all the tools together, get a tool set that comes in a zippered carrying case.

 Save all the paperwork that comes with your computer.

Keep the documents that come with your computer in an accessible place, along with the paperwork from your other computer-related purchases. To keep different-sized documents together, consider putting them in a manila file folder, large envelope, or sealable plastic bag.

 Record the serial numbers of all your equipment and software.

Write the serial numbers of your equipment and software on the outside of the manuals packaged with these items. As noted in the next section, you also should create a single, comprehensive list that contains the serial numbers of all your equipment and software.

 Complete and mail your equipment and software registration cards or register online.

When you register your equipment and software, the vendor usually enters you in its user database. Being a registered user not only can save you time when you call with a support question, it also makes you eligible for special pricing on software upgrades.

 Keep the shipping containers and packing materials for all your equipment.

Shipping containers and packing materials will come in handy if you have to return your equipment for servicing or must move it to another location.

 Identify device connectors.

At the back or front of your computer, you will find a number of connectors for your printer, monitor, mouse, telephone line, and so forth (Figure 63). If the manufacturer has not identified them for you, use a marking pen to write the purpose of each connector on the back or front of the computer case, or photograph or draw the connectors and label them in a notebook.

 Keep your computer area clean.

Avoid eating and drinking around your computer. Also avoid smoking, because cigarette smoke can damage floppy disk drives and floppy disk surfaces.

Check your home or renter's insurance policy.

Some renter's insurance policies have limits on the amount of computer equipment they cover. Other policies do not cover computer equipment at all if it is used for business. In this instance, you may want to obtain a separate insurance policy.

FIGURE 63 Adapter cards have a connector that is positioned in the back of the computer when the card is inserted in an expansion slot on the motherboard.

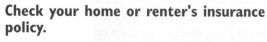

HOW TO MAINTAIN YOUR COMPUTER

Even with the most sophisticated hardware and software, you may need to do some type of maintenance to keep your computer working properly. You can simplify and minimize the maintenance by following the steps listed in this section.

 Start a notebook or file using a simple outline that includes information about your computer.

Keep a notebook that provides a single source of information about your entire computer, both hardware and software and network connectivity. Each time you make a change to your computer, such as adding or removing hardware or software or altering computer parameters, record the change in your notebook. Include the following items in your notebook:

- Vendor support numbers from your user manuals

- Serial numbers of all equipment and software

- User IDs, passwords, and nicknames for your ISP or OSP, network access, Web sites, and so on

- Vendor and date of purchase for all software and equipment

- Trouble log that provides a chronological history of equipment or software problems

- Notes on any discussions with vendor support personnel

Figure 64 provides a suggested outline for the contents of your Computer Owner's Notebook.

 Before you work inside your computer, turn off the power and disconnect the equipment from the power source.

Working inside your computer with the power on can affect both you and the computer adversely. In addition, before you touch anything inside the computer, you should touch an unpainted metal surface, such as the power supply. Doing so will help discharge any static electricity that could damage internal components. As an added protection, for less than $10 from an electronics or computer store, buy an antistatic wristband to prevent static electricity from damaging the computer's circuitry while you replace components. Do not twist, bend, or force components into place. Gently work around existing cables.

Keep the area surrounding your computer dirt and dust free.

Reducing the dirt and dust around your computer will reduce the need to clean the inside of your computer. If dust builds up inside the computer, remove it carefully with compressed air and a small vacuum. Do not touch the components with the vacuum.

FIGURE 64 To keep important information about your computer on hand and organized, use an outline such as this sample outline.

OUTLINE FOR COMPUTER OWNER'S NOTEBOOK

1. List of Vendors
Vendor
Product(s)
City/State
URL
E-mail address
Telephone number
Technical support telephone number

2. Internet and online services information
Service provider name
URL
E-mail address
Logon telephone number
Alternate logon telephone number
Technical support telephone number
User ID
Password

3. Serial numbers
Product
Manufacturer
Serial number

4. Hardware purchase history
Date
Product
Manufacturer
Vendor
Cost
Warranty information

5. Software purchase history
Product
Manufacturer
Vendor
Cost
Date purchased
Date installed/uninstalled
Product keys/registration numbers

6. Trouble Log
Date
Time
Problem
Resolution

7. Support Calls
Date
Time
Company
Contact
Problem
Comments

8. Vendor paperwork

Back up important files and data.

Use a utility program included with the operating system or from a third-party to create a recovery or rescue disk to help you restart your computer if it crashes. Regularly copy important data files to disks, tape, or another computer.

Protect your computer from viruses.

You can protect your computer from viruses by installing an antivirus program and then periodically updating the program by connecting to the manufacturer's Web site. Also, never open a file from an unknown user, particularly those received as e-mail attachments.

Keep your computer tuned.

Most operating systems include several computer utilities that provide basic maintenance functions. In Windows, for example, these utilities are available via the System Tools submenu on the Accessories submenu. One important utility is the disk defragmenter, which allows you to reorganize files, so they are in contiguous (adjacent) clusters, making disk operations faster (Figure 65). Some programs allow you to schedule maintenance tasks for times when you are not using your computer. If necessary, leave your computer on at night so it can run the required maintenance programs. If your operating system does not provide the tools, you can purchase a stand-alone utility program to perform basic maintenance functions.

Learn to use diagnostic tools.

Diagnostic tools help you identify and resolve problems, thereby helping to reduce your need for technical assistance. Diagnostic tools help you test components, monitor resources such as memory and processing power, undo changes made to files, and more. As with basic maintenance tools, most operating systems include diagnostic tools; you also can purchase or download many stand-alone diagnostic tools.

Conserve energy wherever possible.

A simple way to conserve energy is to avoid animated screen savers, which use additional power and prevent your computer from going into hibernation. Fortunately, many of the recent computer, monitor, and printer models go into a very low power mode when not in use for a few minutes. If your printer does not go into a very low power mode, then keep it turned off until you need to print a document or report. Finally, shut your computer system down at night and turn off the main switch on your surge protector.

FIGURE 65 The Disk Defragmenter utility defragments the hard disk by reorganizing the files, so they are in contiguous (adjacent) clusters, making disk operations faster.

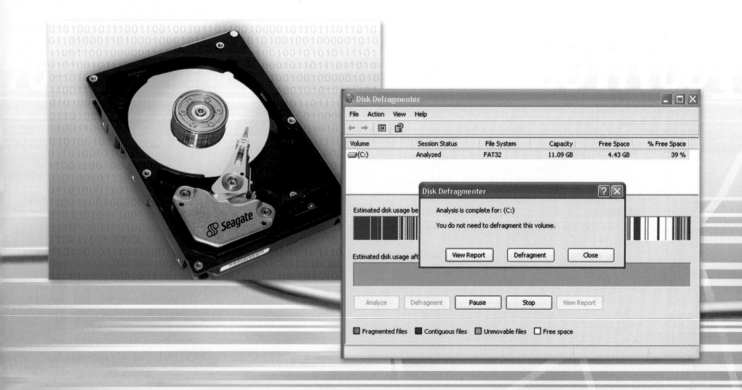

Learn It Online

INSTRUCTIONS

To complete these exercises, start your browser, click the Address box, and then enter scsite.com/ic5/exs.htm. When the Introduction to Computers Web page displays, follow the instructions in the exercises below.

1. Project Reinforcement - True/False, Multiple Choice, and Short Answer

Click Project Reinforcement. Print the quiz by clicking Print on the File menu. Answer each question. Write your first and last name at the top of each page, and then hand in the printout to your instructor.

2. Practice Test

Click Practice Test. Answer each question, enter your first and last name at the bottom of the page, and then click the Grade Test button. When the graded practice test displays on your screen, click Print on the File menu to print a hard copy. Continue to take practice tests until you score 80% or better. Hand in a printout of the final practice test to your instructor.

3. Who Wants to Be a Computer Genius?

Click Computer Genius. Read the instructions, enter your first and last name at the bottom of the page, and then click the PLAY button. Submit your score to your instructor.

4. Wheel of Terms

Click Wheel of Terms. Read the instructions, and then enter your first and last name and your school name. Click the VERY HIGH SCORES link to see other student scores. Close the HIGH SCORES window. Click the PLAY button. Submit your score to your instructor.

5. Crossword Puzzle Challenge

Click Crossword Puzzle Challenge. Read the instructions, and then enter your first and last name. Click the PLAY button. Work the crossword puzzle. When you are finished, click the Submit button. When the crossword puzzle re-displays, click the Print button. Hand in the printout to your instructor.

6. Using the Web Guide

Click Web Guide. Click the Computers and Computing link, and then take a tour of the Virtual Museum of Computing. When you are finished, close the window, and then use your word processing program to prepare a brief report on your tour. Visit four other Web sites listed in the Web Guide and print the main page of each. Hand in the printouts to your instructor.

7. Visiting Web Link Sites

Visit 10 of the 18 Web Link sites in the margins of pages COM-2 to COM-18. Print the main Web page for each of the 10 Web sites you visit and hand them in to your instructor.

8. Scavenger Hunt

Click Scavenger Hunt. Print a copy of the Scavenger Hunt page; use this page to write down your answers as you search the Web. Hand in your completed page to your instructor.

9. Search Sleuth

Click Search Sleuth to learn search techniques that will help make you a research expert. Hand in your completed assignment to your instructor.

INDEX

PHOTO CREDITS

Page 1a Courtesy of Intel Corporation; *Page 1b* Photo courtesy of Iomega Corporation; *Page 1c* Courtesy of International Business Machines Corporation; *Page 1d* Courtesy of Microsoft® Corporation; *Page 1e* Courtesy of Handspring, Inc; *Figure 1a* Courtesy of Dell Computer Corporation; *Figure 1b* Courtesy of Logitech, Inc.; *Figure 1c* Courtesy of Hewlett-Packard Company; *Figure 1d* Courtesy of Telex Communications, Inc.; *Figure 1e* Courtesy of SanDisk; *Figure 1f* Courtesy of SanDisk; *Figure 1g* Courtesy of Hewlett-Packard Company; *Figure 1h* Photo Courtesy of Linksys; *Figure 3* © Scott Goodwin Photography; *Figure 4* Courtesy of Logitech, Inc.; *Figure 5a* Courtesy of Palm, Inc., Palm is a trademark of Palm, Inc.; Figure 5b © 2002 PhotoDisc; *Figure 6* Courtesy of Microsoft® Corporation; *Figure 7* Courtesy of International Business Machines Corporation; *Figure 8* Courtesy of Intel Corporation; *Figure 11 collage* Inkjet printer and output pictures provided by Epson America, Inc.; *Figure 12* Courtesy of Hewlett-Packard Company; *Figure 13* Courtesy of ViewSonic Corporation; *Figure 14a* Courtesy of Dell Computer Corporation; *Figure 14b* Courtesy of ViewSonic Corporation; *Figure 14c* Courtesy of Sony Electronics Inc.; *Figure 14d* Courtesy of Handspring, Inc.; *Figure 14e* Siemens press photo © Siemens AG, Munich/Berlin; *Figure 19* Photo courtesy of Iomega Corporation; *Figure 17b* Courtesy of International Business Machines Corporation; *Figure 20a* Courtesy of International Business Machines Corporation; *Figure 20b* © Scott Goodwin Photography; *Figure 22* Courtesy of International Business Machines Corporation; *Figure 23* Courtesy of Seagate Removable Storage Solutions LLC; *Figure 24a* Courtesy of SanDisk; *Figure 24b* Courtesy of Palm, Inc., Palm is a trademark of Palm, Inc.; *Figure 24c* Courtesy of SanDisk; *Figure 24d* Courtesy of SanDisk; *Figure 24e* Courtesy of SanDisk; *Figure 26* © Scott Goodwin Photography; *Figure 35a* Courtesy of International Business Machines Corporation; *Figure 35b* Courtesy of Dell Computer Corporation; *Figure 35c* Courtesy of ViewSonic Corporation; *Figure 35d* Courtesy of Palm, Inc., Palm is a trademark of Palm, Inc.; *Figure 46* © 2002 Acer, Inc.; *Figure 47* Courtesy of Toshiba America; *Figure 48* Courtesy of Toshiba America; Figure 49 © Jon Feingersh/ CORBIS; *Figure 50* © 2002 Acer Inc.; *Figure 53* AP/ Wide World Photos; *Figure 55* Courtesy of Fujitsu PC Corporation; *Figure 56* Courtesy of Sony Electronics, Inc.; *Figure 57* Courtesy of Compaq Computer Corporation; *Figure 59* Courtesy of Handspring, Inc.; *Figure 65* Courtesy of Seagate Technology LLC.